HEALING
with
CRYSTALS

Pamela Louise Chase
and
Jonathan Pawlik

NEW PAGE BOOKS
A division of The Career Press, Inc.
Franklin Lakes, NJ

HEALING WITH CRYSTALS
Edited by Robert M. Brink
Typeset by Stacey A. Farkas
Cover design by Cheryl Finbow
Printed in the U.S.A. by Book-mart Press

To order this title, please call toll-free 1-800-CAREER-1 (NJ and Canada: 201-848-0310) to order using VISA or MasterCard, or for further information on books from Career Press.

The Career Press, Inc., 3 Tice Road, PO Box 687,
Franklin Lakes, NJ 07417
www.careerpress.com
www.newpagebooks.com

Library of Congress Cataloging-in-Publication Data

Chase, Pamela.
    Healing with crystals / by Pamela Chase and Jonathan Pawlik.—2nd ed.
      p. cm.
    Originally published under the title: Newcastle guide to healing with crystals.
    Includes bibliographical references and index.
    ISBN 1-56414-535-2 (pbk.)
      1. Crystals—Therapeutic use. 2. Quarts crystals—Therapeutic use. 3.
Healing—Miscellanea. I. Pawlik, Jonathan. II. Chase, Pamela. Newcastle
guide to healing with crystals. III. Title.

RZ415 .C43 2001
615.8'9—dc21
                                        2001022220

Acknowledgments

We lovingly acknowledge and thank Katryn LaVanture and Karen Williams for their special support, as well as our other friends in Harrisburg, Pennsylvania, who have shared their crystal experiences and their personal journeys with us. We give special thanks to the fine people at New Page Books for their talents in birthing, and to Robert M. Brink for editing this book. Finally, we thank the crystals, which have patiently taught us so much.

Contents

Part Two: Healing with Quartz Crystals

List of Illustrations

PREFACE

Jonathan is a "stone person." Stone people often had rock collections when they were children and loved to browse on beaches collecting shells and beautiful pebbles. They may carry stones in their pockets for "good luck." While walking in the forest they love to intently examine the smooth rocks in the bottom of streambeds. If you show them your precious gemstone jewelry their eyes light up with excitement, as they are probably collectors as well. Jonathan's natural interest and love of minerals was given a new focus some years ago when he was exposed to books on the metaphysical and healing properties of gemstones.

I, on the other hand, am a "plant person." Trees, wildflowers, and gardens are a major source of comfort and inspiration for me. In the beginning it was hard for me to sense the energies of crystals. Jonathan would hand me a crystal and say, "Do you sense the quiet energy?" and I would respond, "I don't feel anything." Frustration would build up inside. Gradually, with Jonathan's loving patience, I learned how to sense subtle energies, with the crystals acting as the catalyst in the process.

Healing with Crystals describes our growth with this unique mineral and the ways that we personalized our relationship with crystals. Our book is also about healing. My search for understanding and peace of mind has been through the heart, with years of therapy, peer counseling, and learning from life-changing experiences. The fruit of all that work seems to be an understanding and application of the healing process, which can be shared with others.

Our marriage has also been about healing. This book was born of our creative energies and a desire to be of service to others. The process of conceiving this book has been unique. First, Jonathan would receive channeled information and then we would integrate the new knowledge into our healing and counseling work. Our process has been to learn step-by-step. This has allowed us to develop our intuitive skills in such a way that we can teach it to others.

The material in the text that is in "quotes" and in this typeface has been channeled through Jonathan by the Crystal Devas and from the guides that work with him. Every living thing in creation has an evolving consciousness, which is part of the greater consciousness that we call God. Your "higher self" is that part of your consciousness that is aware of its connection with God and can be contacted as a spiritual advisor. You are a particular form or aspect of your Godself, living on planet Earth to learn a particular set of lessons about the greater consciousness.

Devas are the "higher selves" for the kingdoms of Nature. They are the architects for the physical forms that we see. Because they are not separate from the greater consciousness or God, they are teachers of love and understanding. The kingdoms of Nature evolve through giving love and service just as we do. The kingdoms of Nature wish to work with us in a co-creative capacity, which requires a radical shift in our current state of awareness.

We have come to better understand that each one of us receives information in different ways and we incorporate those perceptions into our own belief systems. Therefore, there is no "right way" to work with crystals. What we share here is our own experience, and you can incorporate what is relevant into your own ways of working and perceiving.

Do not assume that if we say something that contradicts your own perceptions, it means that one of us is "wrong." Trust your perceptions and know that you are guided in your own process of learning as we all are. This process takes patience and practice. We hope you will learn to see crystals and other forms of life with new eyes.

—Pamela Chase

INTRODUCTION

P rominently displayed among the crystals in my personal collection is a huge, single-pointed beauty with six sides sitting on a flat base. When I dare to think of its birth, and the cons of time which have passed during its journey from its natural origins to the comfortable library shelf it presently calls home, I am in awe. Still, I find it difficult to grasp the full concept of its nature. The vital and compelling energy of crystal, as well as its inherent healing qualities, perpetually exists in its living presence. Containing the "God essence," it radiates a unique and beneficial power that man is just now rediscovering.

In this book, Pamela Chase and Jonathan Pawlik give a sensitive introduction to the ancient and modern use of crystals as tools for spiritual, mental, and physical healing. The authors offer a new mode of interpretation for the study of crystals. They reveal a clear, simple, and effective process for learning which provides techniques and practical applications. Their unique and relaxing style gives the reader a warm and enlightening experience. While sitting in my den reading this book, I felt that I could hear the "stone person" (Jonathan) discussing the qualities and uses of the various crystals. Sitting opposite in the large leather chair, I could see the "plant person" (Pamela) handling the crystals lovingly as they both brought the book to life.

I hope the reader will use this book to further expand his or her knowledge. The authors present a broad path here. This path allows the reader to explore the fascinating world of crystals. Many in-depth works have been written on the special aspects and uses of crystal. There is so much currently known and so much still unknown about crystals that no one book can encompass the subject. This book is a good key for unlocking the door of the reader's curiosity about the mystery of crystal healing.

In recent years the research of esoteric scholars has gradually removed the dust of ages which had obscured the ancient knowledge of crystals. Consequently, we are now being exposed to the powerful and forgotten healing therapies associated with the quartz crystal. Various esoteric procedures are being improved upon by the additional power of the quartz crystal. Crystal energy is being utilized in the development of exciting new techniques for healing and consciousness expansion. Its potential uses are vast and diverse. Esoteric scholars are now finding that each type of crystal has its own unique vibratory energy, and that each vibratory energy has its corresponding individual properties. The current use of crystals represents yet another significant revival of an ancient esoteric science.

Acquiring your first crystal can be an exciting and time-consuming endeavor. Many people feel compelled to buy a crystal because of its beauty and apparent magnetism. This is meaningful! If you are strongly drawn or attracted to a crystal, I feel this is sufficient reason to make your decision.

It has been written that the crystal was used profusely in Atlantis. The many ways it was used, however, have not yet been fully revealed. Now it appears that Atlanteans are in the process of coming together once again! Could this be the reason why you are a crystal enthusiast? I wonder. Could this be the reason you are filling your personal bookshelf with books about crystals? Are you beginning to open up to past knowledge? Are you looking for the key? These somewhat provocative questions may alert your present-day consciousness to a hidden well of knowledge which you brought with you in this lifetime. Consider these things—your own interest may uncover yet another valuable part of the magnificent crystal puzzle.

There is a deep sense of order and tranquility in this work that I feel is a welcome contribution to the ever-expanding knowledge of crystals. At this point I am tempted to draw upon a metaphor from music. Imagine if you will, a "20th century esoteric symphony of life." This book could be then seen as a "variation on a theme" which allows us to "see" and "hear" a "crystal healing overture" through the sensitive and harmonious efforts of Pamela Chase and Jonathan Pawlik.

—Eileen Connolly

PART 1

Understanding
Quartz Crystals

Chapter 1

The Crystal Bridge to Personal Transformation

The Greek word for crystal, "krystallos" means "clear ice." We don't know whether the concept of "solidified ice" was their literal or their metaphorical understanding. However, we do know that the term "krystallos" originally referred only to clear quartz crystal. In time, the term was applied in a more general way to any solid, symmetrical mineral, transparent or opaque, bounded by plane surfaces. This is how ruby, sapphire, amethyst, and other minerals came to be called crystals. In this book we focus our attention only on natural, clear quartz crystal, as its special properties give it more versatility then any other mineral. When we use the term "crystal" in this book, we are referring to clear quartz crystal.

In this chapter we will become acquainted with the crystal by first looking at some of its physical properties and uses. Then we will examine the "spiritual properties" of crystals, which are those qualities that cannot be measured scientifically.

Physical Properties of Crystal and Its Uses in Technology

Clear quartz crystal consists of molecules of silicon dioxide arranged in a highly structured geometric pattern. The molecules of silicon and oxygen are surrounded by a relatively vast open space, which can be compressed and expanded by certain stimuli, or, in other words, made to vibrate. It is through this property that vibratory energies of different frequencies can be stored in crystals. Scientists have used crystals to store sound, light, and electrical frequencies in computers.

The crystal's highly ordered structure has the ability to be constant, coherent, and reliable in its energy vibrations. For this reason, radio, television, and other devices have their frequency controlled and directed by crystal oscillators. This may also be the reason why crystals are used to focus energy in lasers.

If you tap a crystal with a mallet, you can observe a brief flash of visible light, demonstrating the piezoelectric (pi e´ zo) property of crystals. This property enables the crystal to transform a mechanical pressure into another form of energy such as light, electricity, or sound and then to amplify it. In a record player, for example, the needle is connected to a crystal element and rides in the record grooves. As the needle fluctuates, the mechanical stresses are connected to an electrical signal, which is then amplified into sound.

Clear quartz crystal is used in the optical lenses of precision equipment because of its ability to transmit a greater range of the light spectrum with less distortion than glass. Therefore, we can see that crystal has the proven capabilities of storing, focusing, transmitting, transforming, and amplifying energy.

Life Force Energy and the Energy of Thought

We have looked at the properties of the crystal in terms of energy that can be measured. Now we will expand our definition of energy and take a look at its "spiritual properties." Once we begin to look at reality as an energy system, we are better able to understand the spiritual properties of crystal and its use in healing and consciousness expansion.

Physicists Albert Einstein and Nikola Tesla said that we are surrounded by a "sea of energy" which they described as invisible, boundless, and in perfect order. Physicists now define it as "zero point energy." It is the energy that exists prior to its materialization in form. This energy has been described by a number of earlier scientists. Mesmer called it animal magnetism, Reich called it "orgone," and the 18th century scientist Baron von Reichenbach called it "odic force." This energy was called "prana" in the Hindu tradition and "chi" in the Chinese tradition. It has been described in the eastern spiritual traditions as pure consciousness. In this book we will call it "life force energy," the "raw stuff" out of which we are made.

On the physical level, life force energy ultimately becomes matter. On the spiritual level, life force energy becomes pure consciousness. When we feel a sense of infinite joy, peace, and love, we are experiencing the spiritual aspect of life force energy.

Life force energy is also known to have healing qualities. The Chinese system of acupuncture is based on the flow of chi energy through the body. The ancient Indian system of Ayurvedic medicine utilizes prana as a healing force. The simple truth is that if we are able to incorporate more life force energy into our being on all levels, we will be healthier, happier, and more spiritually attuned. In healing work we are essentially transforming the unmanifested life force energy into manifestations of energy that can nourish and promote our well-being.

Using the analogy of life force energy as a "sea of energy," we are now ready to introduce the first of three key concepts to understanding the function of energy in healing. Thoughts are a form of life force energy. This idea has appeared in many forms throughout the world for thousands of years. In the Bible it is stated, "In the beginning was the Word, and the Word was with God, and the Word was God" (John 1:1). The original "Word" represents the absolute, focused, creative power of Divine energy. In comparison, our normal everyday thoughts lack this special focused power. We can describe our mundane, fleeting thoughts as weakly organized life force energy patterns that register like tiny ripples in this "sea" and then disappear. On the other hand, the additional force of focused will, or strong feeling, adds structure and energy to thought, creating a thought form. This thought form could be described as a specific patterned energy field, which perpetuates itself as a continuous wave in our "sea of energy."

I had an incredible power-of-thought experience several years ago—I was able to dissolve small clouds in the sky with a concentrated thought form or visualization. I got this visualization exercise from Richard Bach's book, *Illusions*. The first time I tried it, I sat down outside and chose a small group of clouds in the sky at which I could direct my thoughts. I visualized a hot laser beam evaporating the cloud and then a dry wind dissolving any leftover particles. This visualization took about three minutes. Part of me was afraid it wouldn't work, and another part of me was afraid of the implications if it did work. Sure enough, the cloud disappeared. It appeared that the structured energy of the thought form reorganized the cloud to be in harmony with the thought pattern.

Once we understand that our thoughts influence our physical reality, then we can become involved in the process of monitoring, changing, or fine-tuning them. This is the point where clear quartz crystal can enhance this process.

We shall now explore the second key to understanding the nature of reality as an energy system. Everything in nature, including the human body, has an energy field. Our bodies do not stop with our physical form. We are essentially a field of energies, which vibrate at different frequencies. Our physical body is surrounded by finer, more subtle frequencies of energy called the aura.

The aura can be sensed in various ways, and can be read as a "printout" of our thoughts. This printout can be visually perceived as changing colors or intuitively sensed as areas of even or uneven flows of energy. We refer to uneven flows of energy as holes or dense spots. By examining our auric fields at any given time, we can determine the nature of our thoughts and feelings, as well as their effects on our physical bodies. It is important to realize that change begins with our thoughts. We can creatively experiment with changing our thoughts and monitoring our progress by checking our energy fields. Symptoms and illnesses in our physical bodies, as they mirror the results of our thoughts, also serve as excellent biofeedback devices for learning about our thought patterns and belief systems.

A third basic concept upon which crystal healing and other healing systems are based, is that we can ultimately affect the health of our physical bodies, as well as our emotional, mental and spiritual states, by changing the energy field surrounding the body. In our work we use healing thoughts, our understanding of energy, and various other tools to balance the energy field. During a healing session the auric field becomes clearer and the holes and dense spots even out. This creates an ideal environment in which to move toward change, growth, and optimal health. The key here is our free will. If we so choose, we can use our free will to block any changes in our energy field. On the other hand, if we choose to align our will and thoughts with a balanced energy field, it becomes easier to move into new levels of well-being and spiritual expansion. Thoughts influence energy, and energy influences thought. By changing our thoughts we can change our energy fields, and by changing and balancing our energy fields we can alter our thoughts.

Non-Physical or Spiritual Properties of Quartz Crystal

We have seen examples of how clear quartz crystal can amplify, transmit, focus, transform, and store electricity and sound energy in technology. Clear quartz crystal can also perform these very same functions with our thought and feeling energy.

Clear quartz crystal amplifies our intuitive, right-brain thoughts and perceptions, helping to increase our awareness of our intuitive language. I have learned about my own dominant modes of intuitive sensing through working with crystals. I tend to intuit through my feelings and internal sense perceptions, such as a sense of open energy flow, or a painful sense of pressure. You may personally discover a more vivid sense of color, a more detailed sense of imagery, and an increased awareness of sound. You may also experience a heightened sense of the energy flow in the body or refined tactile and kinesthetic sensations. You may even notice a greater sensitivity to receiving subtle mental impressions.

Clear quartz crystal transmits the healing qualities of life force energy and the light spectrum throughout our energy system. The healing qualities of color are just beginning to be rediscovered. The clarity of crystal makes it an ideal transmitter and amplifier of color in healing work.

The practice of focusing thought and receiving energy through a crystal for healing purposes is discussed in greater detail in Chapter 5 (Programming Your Crystals).

Clear quartz crystals are a balanced form of energy, which has the ability to help transform an unbalanced field. It seems that the tendency of energy is to move from imbalance to balance or from disorder to order. Therefore, when a more balanced field of energy (like a crystal) comes in contact with a less balanced field of energy (like a stressed-out you), your energy system will move toward balance and you will feel more energized.

Clear quartz crystal also has a unique ability to store thought forms, which can be retrieved at a later time through meditation. The same highly ordered structure that has "room" for electrical sound and light frequencies also has room for thought frequencies. When you program a crystal you may notice that its energy changes. This ability to maintain a new level of energy is due to the crystal's modified internal structure.

Clear quartz crystal shares its gift of communication by acting as both a transformer and a catalyst in helping us to perceive other levels of reality and to understand our total spiritual nature.

A Historical Perspective

We are now only beginning to understand what the ancients knew centuries ago: crystals play an important role in the evolution of society and human consciousness. Seeking spiritual understanding through religious practices has been an integral part of society in most cultures, including Western civilization, up until about four hundred years ago. The spiritual and physical aspects of nature were studied as one unit. The study of the stars included astronomy and astrology. Pythagoras developed mathematical principles that we still use today, as well as the principles that are basic to numerology, the sacred science of numbers. For Pythagoras, numbers had spiritual and physical properties. We are now becoming reacquainted with this idea as we study pyramid energies. Spiritual understanding of the universal laws comes to us through right-brain intuitive functions. It is interesting to note the lack of value placed upon the intuitive mode of knowledge in modern Western civilization.

In tribal cultures, the shamans, or medicine men and women, served as doctors, teachers, and spiritual leaders. They were responsible for the health of the tribe at all levels. Shamans of every culture have used quartz crystal as a sacred power object in their medicine bags.

In ancient China, Taoist priests guarded the caverns where crystals were found. The crystal caves were associated with sacred mountains having mystical properties, and were used in initiation rites. Disciples were led to a special stone bed where the guardian spirit of the cave gave them a dream. Also, according to Kenneth Cohen in *Bones of Our Ancestors,* both the Japanese and Chinese have used crystal balls for contemplation for centuries.[1] Clear quartz crystal has been held in wide respect by many diverse peoples over many years.

There has been a lot of information channeled, or intuitively received, about the Atlantean civilization, that began 50,000 years ago and allegedly sank about 12,000 B.C. The channeling described the integral part that crystals played in the technology and health of the Atlantean civilization. In her article, *"Counseling with Crystals,"* Judith Larkin, Ph.D., described some ways crystals were used, as revealed through past life regressions:

"Crystals were used throughout Atlantean society. They were used as a central energy source for cities. A large crystal ball, thirty feet in diameter or larger, was located (some say suspended) under a pyramid-shaped roof. When meditated upon by specially trained persons, the crystal ball radiated energy much like a central electricity or nuclear energy plant, to power the entire city. The energy was absorbed outside the pyramid room by disc-shaped saucers and directed to specific areas of the town. Power crystals for large cities were immense, sometimes one or two miles in length. Crystals of this large size were not spherically shaped, but were housed under pyramid or dome-shaped roofs.

"In addition to the power crystal, there was a master crystal for each city or territory. The crystal was programmed to protect the area from negative shifts in the planetary energy fields from astrological and social influences. With the use of this balancing master crystal, potential outbreaks of violence could be counteracted. For example, the often-disturbing energies of the full moon could be calmed. Possible volcanic eruptions could be stabilized. The balancing master crystal bathed inhabitants in a soothing flow of energies conducive to human well-being, peace, and a sense of security.

"In addition to being sources of power and balancers of social energy, crystals were also used in Atlantean libraries. The libraries, rather than containing books, had their records imprinted in crystal plates or discs. The crystal plates carried a particular energy or vibration that children and students were taught to interpret psychically much the way North American Indian tribes listened to the rocks talk and tell them stories of the planet's history and human events....

"Communications in general in Atlantean times were nondiscursive and psychic in nature. Crystals were used in schools to teach children how to focus, amplify and transmit their thoughts without the need for vocalization....

"Students were also taught, through the use of the crystal, how to focus and intensify their energy fields enough to vibrate them faster than the speed of light and to thereby dissolve, dematerialize, and, through thought projection, relocate their bodies, much like the 'beam me up Scotty,' dissolution of the physical body shown in Star Trek. Such 'beaming' was the major mode of transportation in Atlantean times...."[2]

It is generally agreed that the misuse of quartz crystal by those greedy for power ultimately led to the destruction of the Atlantean civilization. "One abuse of the crystal was the implantation of small crystal rectangles in the base of the skull of servants, which were programmed so they would follow their masters' wishes."[3]

Another abuse involved battles for supremacy where specially constructed crystals were placed underground and activated with the sun in a special process. The energy was directed to destroy the temples, simulating earthquake activity.[4]

It has been said that some of the Atlanteans escaped to Egypt, preserving some of their knowledge in the Egyptian teachings. The Great Pyramid at Giza may have been a replica of the great temples of Atlantis. Crystal lasers may have cut the big stones, and the pyramids constructed by using crystal power to levitate the stones. There are psychics who think that much of the ancient knowledge is stored in the pyramids and will be uncovered when we are ready to assimilate the information.

In addition to the pyramids, another unique and beautiful legacy, the "crystal skull," reminds us of how much we have to learn about crystals. There have been several skulls found, and Anna Mitchell Hedges discovered the most perfect skull in 1924 in a Mayan temple in British Honduras. This skull is made from clear quartz crystal lacking any markings to indicate that it was carved. It has light pipes, prisms, and lenses within its eye sockets. Scientists are unable to date it, but the skull is considered to be between 20,000 and 500,000 years old. Psychics think it is a memory bank waiting to be decoded.[5]

With the current knowledge and understanding made available about clear quartz crystals, perhaps we now have the opportunity to once again expand our technology, and more importantly our spiritual wisdom, to bring a new level of peace and well-being to our planet.

Shapes of Natural Clear Quartz Crystal

Single-pointed, clear quartz crystal is usually six-sided, with a flat base. Opposite sides are parallel. The base is often cloudy. Energy flows from the base to the point, or termination. The main energy transmissions come from the termination, so it helps if the termination and pyramidal facets are clear and perfect. From now on we will use the common term "point" to refer to the termination.

Sometimes crystals will have mineral inclusions, some of which are known as phantoms. They may also contain internal water or fractures that produce rainbows.

Figure 1-1. Single-pointed clear quartz crystal. Small, clear points are among the most readily available and least expensive forms of crystals. We use them for meditation and healing.

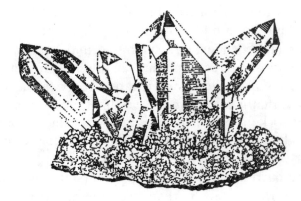

Figure 1-2. Clear quartz crystal clusters. Clusters are single points sharing a common quartz base. Their energy is more diffuse, and they can be used in a variety of ways to create a healing field in a room or on the body. Clusters are also readily available.

Figure 1-3. Double-terminated quartz crystal. Double-terminated crystals are pointed at both ends. Energy flows in two directions like a battery, so these crystals are complete in themselves. Double-terminated crystals are useful in meditation on the third eye or on the crown of the head, and are good for programming. They are also good crystals to place on the body in healing. Unfortunately, they are among the most expensive and least available forms of crystal.

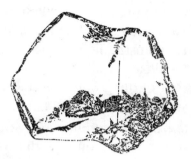

Figure 1-4. Rock crystal. Rock crystal gives a more diffuse energy. It is often cut into different shapes such as balls and pyramids, and can be useful in meditation.

Figure 1-5. Lead crystal. Lead crystal is a special kind of man-made leaded glass, which does not have the specific properties of natural clear quartz crystal.

How Quartz Crystal is Formed

Natural quartz is silicon diozide (SiO_2). It has a hexagonal crystal structure and a hardness of seven on the Mohs' scale. (Diamond, the hardest mineral, has an index of 10.) The earth's crust is roughly 79 percent oxygen and silicon, in various silicate forms. Water is capable of dissolving silicon at about 600 degrees centigrade when under tons of compression. The process is similar to how rock candy crystals are made in a solution of sugar and hot water. The silicon dioxide passes up from deep within the earth and settles in different host rocks, such as granite and sandstone. In most cases, the host rock is also some form of silicate. When silicon dioxide solidifies it bonds with the host silicate, and the crystals grow from the base into their hexagonal shape. If the host rock is not a silicate, such as dolomite, which is a form of calcium magnesium carbonate, then the liquid silicon dioxide does not bond with it. Instead, it crystallizes in all directions, forming double-terminated crystals.[6] Once out of the ground, crystals can be cleaned of surface minerals with oxalic acid.

Points and clusters are mined on a large scale in Arkansas and in Brazil. Fine specimens have been found in the Alps, the Pyrenese, and in Madagascar. Brazil is also well known for its large supply of clear rock crystal.

The Crystal Bridge

A basic key to understanding man's relationship with Nature is the awareness that everything in physical form is a gross manifestation of a subtle and infinitely more beautiful pattern existing in other dimensions. Clear quartz crystal can be seen as a physical manifestation of white light. Because of its clarity the crystal has the capacity to receive and transmit a broad range of frequencies. As we learn to understand and merge with this member of Nature's kingdom, we are led to a greater understanding of its patterns at other levels. The crystal then becomes a bridge to higher wisdom and expanded consciousness.

"Everything on planet Earth exists as an aspect of universal life force energy. You create changing patterns or forms of this energy as you interact with other members of your species and other kingdoms of nature. Energy is in a constant state of change. As you come into contact with higher light beings or expand your consciousness through attunement with the kingdoms of Nature, your vibratory rate changes. Your energy fields receive an influx of light from these sources that expands your sensitivity to the higher self, and to the God consciousness that is present within all life forms. Your personal reality is a product of your beliefs, thoughts, and attitudes about life in general and about yourself in particular. You have free will to determine how open you are going to be to the higher light emanations that seek entrance into your fields of energy to facilitate an elevation in the state of your very soul essence."

Chapter 2

CHOOSING AND CARING FOR QUARTZ CRYSTALS

C hoosing a crystal is a very personal process. Every crystal, as well as every human being, has its own unique energy field.

Some crystals will feel more "energized" than others. In the same way, one crystal will evoke different responses from various people. For this reason, it is important to affirm your own intuition when choosing a crystal. People report feeling "drawn" to the same crystal repeatedly, or that one crystal seems to "speak" to them in some way. Try running your hand above a group of crystals, or hold them and see which ones you enjoy feeling. Trust your sensing and affirm that you are being drawn to the right crystals for you at this time.

In general, look for clarity, especially at the point and the pyramid facets. The points should be as perfect as possible. Any imperfections can diminish the effectiveness of the crystal, and alter the nature of the interaction between the crystal structure and life force energy.

Currently you can find crystals and crystal jewelry that have been symmetrically cut and polished. The use of these crystals is entirely a matter of your beliefs and personal preferences. It is important to work with what attracts you. All other considerations being equal, a large crystal will have more power.

Consider the purposes for your crystals. Smaller ones can be very effective as programmed crystals for meditation, while larger ones can be useful in balancing energies in healing. Crystals are like people—be sensitive and open to the unique gift each has to offer.

Storing Your Crystals

Crystals like to be stored in sunlight and open spaces. They like to be used and enjoyed. Personal crystals can be kept in open, natural containers. Crystals whose purpose is to amplify the energies of an area love to be kept in sunlight. If you want to protect a crystal when carrying it, use natural fabric such as silk or cotton and make sure that the point is protected. You can use black, red, or violet material, or any other color that feels right to you.

If you store a crystal in the dark for a long period of time, it will need to be recharged in sunlight for optimal functioning.

Cleaning Your Crystals

Over a period of time, quartz crystals can collect various forms of negative or static energies such as electronic pollution, negative thought forms and emotions, and loud, inharmonious sounds, as well as imbalanced electromagnetic energies. These imbalanced energies are picked up on the external surface of the crystal, and can affect the emanation of positive vibratory energy. Be aware of the fact that as a crystal balances particularly strong imbalanced energies it may crack or develop inclusions. It is important to clean and charge a crystal when you first obtain it, and frequently thereafter, to keep it at its highest level of functioning.

Take time to check your crystals often to see if they need cleaning.

Some symptoms of a crystal that needs to be cleaned are a sense of decreased energy coming from it, increased cloudiness within it, or stickiness to the touch. There are many ways to clean a crystal, so choose the method that seems right for you.

1. For quick cleaning after healing work or at the end of the day, hold the crystal under cold running water, pointing down, for half a minute or more. You should hold the crystal between both hands. Visualize white light clearing and illuminating the crystal. Thank and love the crystal for its service.

2. Burn dried sage leaves in a piece of pottery or abalone shell. You can buy sage leaves at an herb or health food store. Pass the crystal, point up, through the fragrant smoke, affirming that the crystal is pure and clear. Again, thank and love the crystal. Crystals can be soaked in sage tea. Sage has the ability to both clear and uplift the emotional, mental, and spiritual states, which is one reason why it was used by North American Indians as a purifier at the beginning of spiritual ceremonies.

3. Use your breath to clear the crystal. When you breathe, you inhale and exhale life force energy. For this reason, the breath is a powerful tool for healing. Hold the crystal with your index finger on the largest pyramidal facet and inhale slowly and deeply. Now, hold your breath while you visualize and affirm the imbalanced energies being transformed and the crystal clearing. (Only hold your breath long enough to focus your thoughts. This is not intended to be an uncomfortable process.) Continue this thought visualization process while you exhale slowly through your nostrils onto the crystal. You will need to do this several times until the crystal feels like it has been cleared. Use of the breath with crystal has been thoroughly developed by Marcel Vogel, a former IBM senior research scientist currently doing crystal research.

4. For a more thorough cleaning, we like to place the crystals in a saltwater solution overnight or longer. We have used anywhere from one teaspoon to two tablespoons of sea salt per two cups of spring water, purchased from the grocery store.

5. Crystals can also be buried in sea salt for one to seven days. Sea salt attracts imbalanced energies like a magnet. However, the salt loses its strength as it neutralizes these energies, so the salt water or the sea salt must be thrown away periodically.

6. Crystals can be placed in the rain with the affirmation that they are being cleared.

7. If a crystal is carrying a particularly strong negative influence, it can be buried under the earth for several days. It is a good idea to ask the devas of the crystal and the earth to help you transform the imbalanced energy so that it doesn't remain in the earth in that state.

Charging Your Crystals

Once crystals have been cleaned and cleared of static, they must be charged with positive energies.

1. Quick charging is possible using the breath. Hold the crystal with the index finger on the pyramidal facet, as in the clearing exercise. Inhale slowly and deeply, hold your breath, and visualize the crystal charged with light, vitality, and love. Continue the visualization while you exhale through your nose in short bursts into the crystal. You will probably need to do this several times.

2. We like to charge crystals by placing them on a white cloth in direct sun for about six hours, and sometimes for a day and night in the full moon.

3. If for some reason six hours of sunlight is not possible, we ask the devas and other spirits, who channel their healing energies through the crystals, to help charge and prepare them for healing use. We visualize the crystals as sparkling and clear and full of sunlight, and affirm that they are being fully charged.

4. We also charge crystals, particularly in inclement weather, by placing them on a crystal cluster or under a pyramid for a day or two. Pendants and other crystals that you carry

with you can be washed and kept on a cluster or under a pyramid overnight, so that they are optimally charged for the next day. Our experience, however, is that they may eventually need to be cleared and recharged by other methods.

5. Crystals can be charged in snowstorms, thunderstorms, and other dynamic weather conditions.

6. Keeping crystals in power spots, such as holy places or energy vortex fields, also charges them.

7. Crystals can be charged using the concentrated affirmation that they are filled with love and life force energy.

Saturation

Our experience has been that, over a period of time, a crystal will absorb imbalanced energy, which diminishes its capacity to generate balanced life force energy. This seems to be particularly true of crystals that you use for healing purposes. One sign to look for is the crystal feeling like it needs to be cleaned, except that cleaning it does not seem to clear and regenerate the energy. Another sign is when a crystal that first felt uplifting or comfortable, begins to feel uncomfortable. When this happens, the crystal has done all it can, and it is time to return it to the earth (or the water).

1. Ask the spiritual consciousness of the crystal whether its work with you has been completed, or whether it has a further purpose in your life.

2. Ask it what element (Earth or Water primarily) will be most beneficial for its internal balance, and take the crystal where it needs to go. Most likely it will be a natural place.

3. When you release the crystal, take a few minutes in meditation to thank it for the service it has given you, and honor your interdependence with the Earth.

Crystals appreciate being treated with care and love. As you work with them, you will become more sensitive to their needs, and they will reward you with expanding awareness.

Chapter 3

EXPLORING THE
POTENTIAL OF CRYSTAL

Familiarizing Yourself with Crystals

W e will now give you some exercises to help you familiarize yourself with crystal energy. These ideas were drawn from Randall and Vicki Baer's *Windows of Light,*[1] as well as from our own work. Exercise 3 introduces you to your sensing hand, the hand in which you feel sensations most strongly. In Exercise 6 we introduce the terms receiving hand and sending hand, which relate to the magnetic polarities of your body. Further explanations of this concept are given in Chapters 6 and 8. We are introducing these terms now in order to help you determine the hand in which you will hold your crystal for healing work. Your sensing hand can be either your sending or receiving hand. We find that it varies from individual to individual.

Exercises

1. Take time to hold the crystal in the light and examine its beautiful facets. Let your imagination find the rainbows and galaxies in your crystal. Appreciate your crystal and thank it for its unique gifts. Then close your eyes and remember as many details as possible about your crystal.

2. It is important to get a sense of how crystal energy feels. Hold your crystal in your left hand for a minute or so with the point toward your body. Be aware of any sensations or reactions. These are subtle sensations so if you don't feel anything at first, don't worry and just keep practicing. Also, notice where you feel reactions in your body. The energy seems to travel to where it is needed, so you may feel a tingling or warm sensation where the balancing is occurring. Now, try holding the crystal in your right hand and see if you notice any differences in the sensations you are receiving. Are the sensations stronger in one hand than in the other?

3. This exercise can help you find out which hand is your sensing hand. This is the hand that you use for sensing the energy in crystals or scanning the energy of another person's body. Your sensing hand is the hand in which you felt the sensations most strongly in the last exercise. Hold your hands about four inches apart as if you are holding an imaginary ball. Now hold the crystal in your right hand with the point facing toward the left palm. Draw circles in the field in front of your left palm. Be aware of the sensations. Repeat with the crystal in the left hand pointing toward the right palm. Your sensing hand will be the one in which the sensations are the most pronounced.

4. Hold the crystal in your left hand with the point toward your body for about thirty seconds. Then place it away from you for the same amount of time. Notice how you can feel the energy in your hand even when the crystal is not present. You may also notice energy building up in your hand or body. Be aware of any other changes.

5. Roll the crystal between your hands. Then hold it still in your left hand with the point toward your body. Repeat with your right hand, and notice the piezoelectric effect, or the amplified strength of the crystal's energy.

6. To find out which is your sending and which is your receiving hand, you will need two crystals. In the healing model which we use, it is important to know which hand has a negative charge (receiving hand) and which hand has a positive charge (sending hand). Hold one crystal in your left hand with the point facing toward the body and the other crystal in your right hand with the point facing away from your body. Sense the flow of energy in your body. Now reverse the crystals so that the crystal in the left-hand points out, and the one in the right hand points in. Sense again. One circuit will probably feel more comfortable than the other will. The hand where the crystal is pointing in toward the body becomes your receiving hand.

    If you don't have two crystals right now, another way you can check this is by using a pendulum (described in the next chapter). From now on we will use the terms "receiving" and "sending." If you are not sure, right-handers can use receiving in reference to their left hand and sending in reference to their right hand. Left-handers can do the reverse.

7. To get an idea of how it feels to work with the crystal on your third eye, hold the crystal in your right hand in front of your third eye with the point away from the forehead. Sense the energy. Now turn the crystal point toward your forehead and notice the difference. When you work with the crystal on your third eye, you will have to lay it on or tape it to your forehead, point up. Use hypoallergenic tape that you can purchase at the drugstore.

8. Now, hold the crystal point away from your third eye and imagine a color. Visualize the crystal as being this color. Concentrate on this image. Turn the crystal point toward your forehead and remain receptive. You can repeat this exercise using forms, images, or feelings.

Meditation with Quartz Crystals

Crystal is very beneficial for meditation. It can help you reach alpha and theta states more quickly and deeply because of its balancing effects. For this reason, simply holding a crystal can be very relaxing. The crystal also amplifies signals from your intuition, helping you to increase awareness of your own intuitive language. If you receive pictures or symbols, you may find them more vivid or prolific, similar to "tuning the picture" on a TV screen. If you receive "energy sensations" and feelings, the subtle distinctions are more clearly perceived, making it easier to hear and sense your own wisdom.

The first step in working with the crystal is to attune it to your energies by holding it. There are several ways you can hold the crystal for meditation. One is to hold it in your receiving hand with the point toward the fingertips. If you wish to feel the concentrated energy from the crystal, the point can face toward you.

Another way to hold it is to cup your hands, placing your receiving hand on the bottom and your sending hand on the top. The crystal sits in your sending hand with the point upwards. It helps if the crystal has a flat base for this. You can also hold or tape the crystal to your third eye, point up. This position seems a little more sensitive than the others do, so watch for dizziness or headaches. Our experience is that once you have adjusted to the increased amplification on your forehead, you will not experience these symptoms. Most of all, you should do what seems right at the time.

Crystals can help calm and focus any meditation practice: sitting, breathing, affirmations, visualizations, etc. You can keep a crystal cluster in your special meditation place to amplify higher energies. Breathing with the crystal helps you to attune to it.

The following simple meditation visualization can help you to relax and amplify your attunement with the Earth:

WHILE HOLDING A CRYSTAL POINT UP IN YOUR CUPPED HANDS, VISUALIZE YOURSELF SITTING IN A FAVORITE NATURAL PLACE. IMAGINE YOU ARE SURROUNDED BY A CIRCLE OF CRYSTALS, POINTS FACING COUNTERCLOCKWISE, WITH SPECIAL ONES POINTING TOWARD YOU AT EACH OF THE FOUR DIRECTIONS.

It may also be helpful to follow this visualization with a meditation for attuning with your crystal:

BECOME AWARE OF HOW YOU ARE FEELING PHYSICALLY, EMOTIONALLY, MENTALLY, AND SPIRITUALLY, AS YOU PREPARE TO SIT WITH YOUR MEDITATION CRYSTAL. TAKE A FEW BREATHS, INHALING SLOWLY, HOLDING FOR A MOMENT, THEN EXHALING SLOWLY. AS YOU HOLD YOUR CRYSTAL, YOU MAY EXPERIENCE A VARIETY OF SENSATIONS SUCH AS TEMPERATURE CHANGES, TINGLING SENSATIONS, OR A SENSE OF EXPANDING PEACE WITHIN YOURSELF. IT IS GOOD NOW TO SIT QUIETLY IN A RECEPTIVE STATE, ALLOWING THE VIBRATIONS OF THE CRYSTAL TO HARMONIZE WITH YOUR VIBRATIONS. WITH THOUGHTS OF PURE LOVE AND LIGHT, ASK YOUR CRYSTAL TO OPEN AN AREA OF ITS STRUCTURE SO THAT YOU MAY ENTER INSIDE ITS PERFECT FORM. OBSERVE HOW YOUR CRYSTAL CREATES A SPECIAL SPACE FOR YOU TO COME WITHIN ITS BEING. ENTER YOUR CRYSTAL NOW THROUGH THE DOORWAY OF LIGHT PROVIDED FOR YOU. FEELING IN A STATE OF PERFECT BALANCE, YOU CHOOSE TO EXPLORE THE INTERIOR OF YOUR CRYSTAL. ALLOW ALL OF YOUR SENSES TO BE OPEN TO EXPERIENCE YOUR CRYSTAL, TOUCH ITS SIDES, ITS FOUNDATIONS WITH YOUR HANDS AND YOUR FACE. ALLOW YOUR BODY TO LEAN AGAINST A CRYSTAL WALL. LISTEN FOR ANY SOUNDS YOU MAY HEAR. FEEL THE SENSE OF BEING AT HOME, BEING TOTALLY WELCOMED BY YOUR CRYSTAL. PAUSE NOW IN STILLNESS FOR A FEW MOMENTS TO ALLOW THE INTEGRATION OF THE ATTUNEMENT. PREPARE NOW TO LEAVE THE CRYSTAL. THANK IT FOR SHARING ITS ENERGIES WITH YOU AND RETURN TO THE PRESENT.

It is important to be patient as you practice. Trust in your abilities to be at one with your higher self. Love yourself unconditionally, releasing fear and doubt. See yourself as crystal clear and filled with sparkling light.

Asking for Intuitive Guidance

The crystal is one of many tools that offer you the opportunity to learn how to listen and to dialogue with your own inner knowing. Developing your intuition is a key in learning how to manifest well-being for yourself, others, and the planet. Here is a way to use your breath and the crystal in order to receive intuitive impressions. This exercise will also center you for further intuitive work. In the following exercise, you will ask the crystal how it would like to be cleaned (See Chapter 2 for ideas). Another simple way to try this exercise is to ask for guidance on an everyday routine or activity, such as "What kind of exercise do I need today?"

1. Sit and hold the crystal in your receiving hand, or lie down and place a crystal on your third eye.

2. Use the breath process of the previous exercise to balance and center yourself.

3. Inhale deeply and ask your question, for example, "What is the best way to clean this crystal?"

4. Pause and hold your breath, keeping your focus on your intent, or a mental picture of your intent. Holding your breath helps to build the power of the life force energy.

5. Exhale, relax, and let the thought go. You may think that it is necessary to keep directing your will in order to manifest intent. A crucial step in working with spirit is to listen, which is the point of relaxing deeply.

6. Pause, and allow information about your question to come to you. If you do not receive the information you asked for the first time, try to release any preconceived ideas about the answer, or about the form the answer might take. Then try again, and create a rhythm of focusing and letting go.

Another way to develop a dialogue with your intuition is by using the pendulum, which we will explore in Chapter 4.

Symbolic Uses of Quartz Crystal

Many cultures use clear quartz crystal as a symbol for light. Most likely it is a spiritual symbol for you also. The power of a symbol is that it can keep your attention focused toward a particular intent, and therefore it strengthens the power of your thought. The most common ways that crystals are used as symbols are:

1. Wearing clear quartz crystal as a pendant or a necklace.

2. Placing a crystal on an altar, or in a particular place where it is visible to you or others.

3. Working with visual images of crystals and symbols containing crystals.

The point we are trying to make here is that the crystal has its own internal energy. It transmits this energy naturally and you can sense it. It can also be a symbol in its relationship to you. Its power as a transmitter and its power as a symbol are two separate but integrated functions. For example, when you wear a crystal for a period of days or months, it eventually becomes saturated (see Chapter 2). However, it can still retain its power as a symbol for a particular intent. The power of symbols is not to be underestimated, and we are still in the beginning stages of understanding the power of the mind to heal.

Chapter 4

The Crystal Pendulum: Contacting Higher Guidance

How to Use the Crystal Pendulum

Pendulums are an excellent tool to help develop your intuition and self-awareness. Essentially, a crystal pendulum can be seen as a biofeedback device for monitoring attunement with your higher self. By listening to your higher self as you go about your daily life, you can also learn to fine-tune your discrimination in energy sensing.

Before using a pendulum, it helps to carry the crystal with you for a few days to attune it to your energy. When you are ready to begin, you can sit down at a table and hold the chain or cord of the pendulum with your thumb, index, and middle fingers. Your elbow should be resting comfortably on the table and your wrist straight. Experiment with the length of the chain or cord. A comfortable length will be approximately between three and twelve inches. In our experience the material of the chain or cord doesn't really matter.

It is very important to be relaxed and centered when using the pendulum. Take a few deep breaths, and visualize a place where you feel totally at peace. Affirm that your higher self is with you. Don't rush this relaxation. If you are not relaxed you will not get clear answers. In the beginning it is easy to become so worried about whether or not the pendulum will work that you can block the movement of the pendulum with your tension.

When you are ready, ask the pendulum to show you the movement for "yes" and the movement for "no." If you get no response, try holding the pendulum over the positive and then negative ends of a battery (not a dead one). You can use the movement over the positive end for "yes" and the movement over the negative end for "no." If this method does not work for you, don't despair. You can decide on a system such as clockwise (yes) and counterclockwise (no), or vertical (yes) and horizontal (no), or a combination of these positions.

Move the pendulum in your "yes" direction, visualizing "yes" in bold letters in your mind, and connecting to the sensation of the "yes" motion. Affirm that this is a "yes." Repeat with the "no" motion. Then ask your pendulum to show you a "yes" or a "no." This may take some practice over a period of time. It took me about two weeks to become comfortable with using the pendulum. Trust that you are learning and persevere until you get a response.

Now you are ready to begin asking questions that can be answered with a "yes" or a "no." When you are working with a pendulum, do not have your arms or legs crossed or touching each other. It is also good to wash your hands before starting. Work on an uncluttered surface, away from electrical equipment and magnets.

Ask your pendulum, "Are we in harmony?" or "Am I in tune with my pendulum?" Readings are easily influenced by fatigue, illness, emotional states of mind, beliefs regarding the question, and any inharmonious energies which may be present. Learning to stay in harmony with your pendulum is one of the most challenging lessons in working with it.

As you receive answers, listen to your "inner voice." Watch for bodily sensations and inner perceptual sensations. We both get an uncomfortable pressure in our hands or an inner sensation of blocked energy when the answer is "no."

You are able to gain additional information by noting the strength of the pendulum's responses, particularly in healing work. In addition, you may be able to receive responses from the pendulum different from your standard yes/no movement. At this time it would be a good idea to ask your pendulum to indicate how it would move to communicate each of the following statements:

1. Now is not the appropriate time to ask that question.
2. I am not in tune with the pendulum.
3. I need to clarify my question and ask it in a different way.

Questions to Ask Your Crystal Pendulum

Now you are ready to use your pendulum in crystal work. Here are questions that can be answered with the pendulum. Ask them in a yes/no format. Some of these questions refer to ways of working with a crystal that will be discussed in later chapters.

Choosing your crystal:

1. "Am I to work with you?" ("You" refers to a crystal.)
2. "Are you to be used in meditation/healing?"

Care of your crystal:

1. There are two ways you can find out whether a crystal needs to be cleaned. One is to hold the pendulum over the crystal and ask the pendulum to show you its relative strength. If you get a "no," the crystal needs to be cleaned. Another way is to ask the crystal "Do you need to be cleaned?"
2. Get a yes/no response for each of the following methods of cleaning crystals to find out how your crystal needs to be cleaned:
    a. Burying in sea salt.
    b. Soaking in sea salt water.
    c. Holding in sage smoke.
    d. Breathing on it.
    e. Putting crystal out in the rain.
    f. Holding crystal under running water.
    g. Burying crystal underground.

3. When you have had some practice with the pendulum, you can make an arc, and ask the pendulum to point to the optimal way to clean the particular crystal in the shortest period of time. Using an arc will save you time, as well.

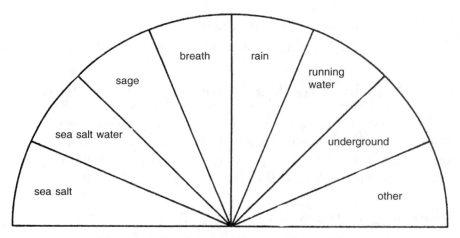

Figure 4-1. Pendulum arc for specific qualities.

4. "Should the crystal be cleaned for four hours, six hours, eight hours, overnight, 24 hours?"
5. Recheck the crystal and ask, "Have you been adequately cleaned?" Sense the crystal with your hand. You can eventually learn by touch when the crystal is clean.
6. Ask: "How is the crystal to be charged?"

    By using:

    a. Affirmations?
    b. Breath?
    c. Sunlight?
    d. On a cluster?
    e. Under a pyramid?
    f. In a thunderstorm?
    g. For how long?

Uses for your crystal:

1. Location in a room: "Would you like to be on the window sill? By the bed? etc."
2. In meditation:
   a. "Am I to sit with you in a totally receptive state?"
   b. "Am I to actively access your memory for specific information?"
   c. "Shall I place you in my receiving hand, on my heart, on my third eye?"

There are some other questions you can ask as you work with programming your crystals and using them for healing. These questions will be included in later chapters. However, you can already see the kind of clarification you can receive by using the pendulum.

Another kind of arc you can use with the pendulum is called the "confidence arc." This helps you to fine-tune the strength of a response.

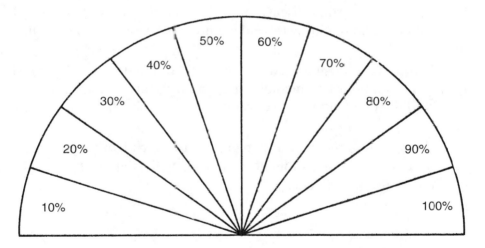

Figure 4-2. Confidence arc for pendulum.

For example, you can measure various crystals for use in meditation and to find out which one will be the strongest for you at this time. We have learned a great deal about our personal crystals through dialoguing with our pendulums.

Determining Your Sending and Receiving Hands

We now return to the question of determining your sending and receiving hands. We have observed that if you hold the pendulum over the North Pole of a magnet (We used a one-inch neodymium magnet), the pendulum rotates clockwise. The pendulum rotates counterclockwise over the South Pole.

To determine your sending and receiving hands, you can hold the pendulum over your left, and then your right palm and ask, "What is the direction of energy flow in this hand?" If the rotation is clockwise, then that is your sending hand.

If you have two magnets, you can try holding one in each hand. Turn the North Pole facing in toward your palm in one hand, and the South Pole facing in toward your palm in the other hand. Sense the comfort level of energy flow in your hands, and the energy flow in your body, and then turn the magnets over so that you reverse the polarity. One circuit will feel more comfortable and promote greater energy flow. The hand with the North Pole facing in toward the palm is your sending hand. There is a further discussion of the sending and receiving hands in Chapter 6, and of clockwise and counterclockwise rotation in Chapter 8.

If you get confusing answers, take time to breathe deeply, detach from your emotions and mental mind, and try again. Another solution is to hold the pendulum over your left palm and ask, "Is this my receiving hand?"

We have found that your perceptions of which hand is your sending hand are somewhat influenced by your beliefs about handedness and how to use your hands.

Chapter 5

PROGRAMMING YOUR CRYSTALS

P rogramming a crystal is a powerful way of bonding with it. The process teaches you more about what it means to co-create with the spiritual consciousness of Nature for healing and transformation. A programmed crystal has the unique ability to amplify and continuously emanate programmed energy. One of my own more graphic experiences has been in working to remember my dreams. When I put a crystal under my pillow and affirmed that I would remember my dreams in the morning, I did indeed remember more of them. However, when I programmed the crystal to amplify my dreams so that I could recall them in the morning, the dreams I remembered were even more complete and vivid.

One way that a crystal becomes programmed with your intention is when you use it repeatedly for a specific purpose, such as meditation or healing. This is the simplest type of programming. When you want a crystal to retain a program over a period of time, it is more effective to program the crystal consciously.

Types of Crystals to Be Programmed

All crystals have a higher purpose to serve. Some crystals are better for meditation, and some are better for different types of healing. Some are here as our "instructors" in interdimensional communication. The first step is to ask the spiritual consciousness of the crystal whether the crystal is optimal for the particular program that you have in mind.

Preparing for Programming

Spend some time with a pencil and paper writing a concise, potent affirmation that is for the "highest good of all concerned." You can ask your pendulum to help you choose your wording. Then ask, "Is this program worded appropriately for my highest good?"

Steps for Programming

1. Hold the crystal in your receiving hand. Center yourself by focusing on inhaling and exhaling. Attune with the crystal by imagining that you are deep under the surface of the earth where rocks are formed, and become One with the crystals deep in the earth. Become aware of your symmetry, and any other impressions that come to you.

2. Cup your sending hand inside your receiving hand, and place the crystal in your sending hand. Ask your crystal to open a part of its matrix to receive the program. It is important to ask permission of the crystal with honor and respect when programming, because you are essentially changing its structure. You can visualize an area of light opening up inside it. Wait receptively and allow your crystal to open. Ask with your pendulum, "Is your matrix adequately opened?" or "Are you prepared to receive the program?"

3. If you are programming color, sound, vibrations of a particular location, or other phenomena, you can put the crystal in an appropriate place and leave it for a period of time. Ask the crystal, "Are you adequately programmed with this vibration?" Go to step 5.

4. For a thought program you can repeat your affirmation three or more times, continuing your visualization and affirmation until you have a sense that you have done enough. Check with the pendulum, asking, "Is this crystal adequately programmed?"

5. Focus your awareness on your breath. Inhale in short, sharp, breaths and contract your abdominal muscles. Exhale Light and Love into the crystal. You are further programming the crystal with your intent.

6. Thank the crystal for assisting you with your highest good. Remain in a meditative state with its energies.

7. Close your meditation.

You are the only person who can remove a program that you have put into the crystal. Cleaning and charging does not erase a program—conscious intent does. To remove a program from a crystal, follow the same process you used to enter the program. Visualize pure white light that erases the program. This is an important step to take before you give away a crystal that you have programmed.

As your life unfolds co-creatively with the mineral kingdom, keep in mind the qualities of trust and patience as you learn more about programming. It is a process of learning how to honor the sacred space that is present within you as well as the sacredness of the crystal. You are developing a relationship that is based on the giving and receiving of mutual honor and trust.

Ideas for Programming Crystals

The main idea here is that you can program a crystal to assist you in deepening your intuitive connection with anything that expands your spiritual understanding. The purpose of these suggestions is to stimulate your own ideas for programming crystals. You can put more than one program in a crystal. Ask whether the program you are considering is appropriate for the crystal. Combine an affirmation or a statement of intent with:

* Color. You can visualize colors, or work with colored lights.

* Sound. Music, environmental sounds, chants, and toning all work well.

* Geometric form. Place the crystal on a mandala or inside a three-dimensional form such as a pyramid.
* Energy vortexes. Take your crystal to sacred places and program it to receive their energies.
* Symbols such as the yin-yang. State your intent and leave it on the symbol for a period of time. Ask the crystal if it has been adequately programmed.
* Dreams.
* Past life experiences.
* Pets and other species communication.
* Gardens and land where you are focusing healing energies.
* Chakras.

Here are some sample affirmations:

"YOU SURROUND ME WITH LIGHT FOR MY HIGHEST GOOD," [Can be a good affirmation for a crystal that you wear or carry.]

FOR THE PHYSICAL BODY: "I AM WHOLE AND HEALED."

FOR THE EMOTIONAL BODY: "YOU ARE A CATALYST FOR BRINGING BLOCKED ENERGIES INTO MY CONSCIOUS AWARENESS FOR RELEASE."

For Colors:

RED: "I MOVE FORWARD IN LIFE WITH COURAGE AND CONFIDENCE. I AM ROOTED AND SECURE."

ORANGE: "I HONOR MY FEELINGS AND MY SENSES."

YELLOW: "I AM MENTALLY CLEAR AND CONFIDENT."

GREEN: "I AM IN BALANCE, FLOW, AND HARMONY WITH MY GROWTH PROCESS."

BLUE: "I MERGE MY WILL WITH DIVINE WILL."

INDIGO: "MY INNER SENSITIVITY TO ALL LIFE IS EXPANDING AND BECOMING CLEARER."

VIOLET: "I AM ONE WITH ALL THAT IS."

FOR MEDITATION: "MY CONNECTION WITH MY HIGHER SELF IS EXPANDING AND BECOMING CLEARER."

"Every crystal has a particular function in life and can gravitate to even greater levels of service and responsibility through the influence of the conscious and subconscious energies emerging from the human kingdom. Whenever the crystal receives a visual imprint into its being, the picture is not only stored within, but is amplified geometrically each time that image is called for from the crystal in a meditation. Greater insights will emerge as you gain a greater awareness of the possibilities the crystal has to work with you."

PART 2

Healing with
Quartz Crystals

Chapter 6

THE HUMAN
ENERGY SYSTEM AND
THE CRYSTAL

Components of the Human Energy System

I n Chapter 1 we introduced the idea that there is an energy field
surrounding our bodies. We call this energy field the aura, and it
consists of patterned layers of energies vibrating at different frequencies. Everything in nature is surrounded by an aura, which serves as a
template, or blueprint, for the physical form. In the 1960s, Russian scientists Semyon and Valentina Kirlian sparked world interest by developing a technique to photograph these energy fields known as Kirlian
photography. One of their most important findings is called the "phan-
tom leaf" effect. After removing a portion of a plant leaf, they were
able to photograph an energy field around the leaf as if the whole leaf
were still present. They concluded that the energy field around the leaf
forms a pattern that acts as an organizing force field for physical matter. The Russians referred to this "organizing field" as the biological
plasma body. Einstein, in his unified field theory, also stressed that the
energy field creates the form If this is true, then we should learn more

about this energy field if we want to effectively heal ourselves on all levels. To do this we must first look at its "non-physical structure."

There is general agreement that the aura consists of a number of layers, or subtle bodies. However, perceptions vary as to the number of subtle bodies and their actual dimensions. Our particular working system roughly defines three layers of subtle bodies corresponding to the physical, emotional, mental, and spiritual levels of development. We combine the emotional and mental levels in our work, since they are both related to the fashioning of conscious beliefs.

The most physical layer is usually called the "etheric," which seems to extend from about one-quarter inch to two or three inches from the physical body. It is sometimes seen as a thin band of white or grayish light, and, being the densest layer, it is the easiest to perceive. When we wear crystals or place them on the body, we are directly affecting the etheric body.

Surrounding the etheric body are the emotional and mental bodies. We are able to sense these layers from about three or four inches to about twelve inches from the body. These fields are often seen clairvoyantly as shimmering and changing colors that indicate the person's emotional and mental state.

From about 12 inches and extending at least another two or three feet from the physical body is the spiritual body. This is the level where we merge with our higher self and feel connected to the reality beyond our conscious everyday knowing.

Our subtle bodies are highly sensitive to thought forms. When a thought form enters one of our subtle bodies, the structure of that body changes to incorporate or resonate with the thought. Depending upon the nature of the thought, the subtle bodies either become more stabilized, structured, and filled with life force energy, or the opposite process occurs and they become more disorganized. This process can happen instantaneously. For this reason, clairvoyants see many colors, some with more predominant overtones, and others more fleeting and changing. It is very important to understand that we structure our very beings with our thoughts. It is also important to recognize that we can affect our sensitive energy fields in very positive ways to bring about balance and well-being.

In addition to serving as a blueprint for the body and as a record for our experiences, the layers or bodies of the aura also serve as transducers of life force energy. We receive life force energy from a variety of sources, including thought. These finer energies are made denser at each level, until they assume a form that our bodies can use.

Another component of the human energy system is the chakras. The word "chakra" comes from Sanskrit, and means "wheels of light," which is what they look like when photographed with Kirlian photography. According to Gabriel Cousens, "The Tibetans refer to these energy centers as 'khor-lo,' which also means wheel.... In the Bible, John refers to these energy centers as the 'seven seals on the back of the book of life...' The Kabbalists refer to these centers as 'the seven centers in the soul of man.' There is obviously a historical cross-cultural tradition among many of the major religions that validates the existence of these subtle energy centers."[1] "These interdimensional chakras can be thought of, metaphorically, as tubes between the subtle bodies. When all subtle bodies are aligned, then all seven interdimensional chakra 'tubes' become synchronized and cosmic energy flows through the body with the least resistance."[2]

A final component of our human energy system is the network of nadis and meridians. The nadis, described in Yoga and Ayurveda, are like spokes of a wheel radiating outward from each chakra, carrying transduced energy into the endocrine system and vital organs. The traditional system of Chinese medicine is based on stimulating the flow of chi through the meridians. These meridians are another system for transporting life force energy—much like a subtle nervous system. The texts of acupuncture describe 12 main organ meridians, eight "extraordinary vessels," and numerous sub-branches. It is possible that the acupuncture points of the Chinese system are the intersections of the nadis and the meridians.

What happens when we introduce crystal energy into the fields of the human energy system? In its natural state, the crystal's energy field is in a state of equilibrium. By definition, a balanced energy field has an abundance of life force energy. When the crystal's energy field has direct contact with our own, life force energy passes into the human energy system. It also follows that the more ways we find to incorporate clear quartz crystals, gemstones, herbs, natural foods, sunshine, fresh air, pets, houseplants, and other forms of nature into our lives, the more healthy and energized we will be.

The Human Body as a Crystal

There are scientists who are interested in finding scientific explanations for how crystals work. Jonathan and I believe that we cannot fully understand crystal healing without exploring the nonphysical or spiritual workings of reality. Nevertheless, the scientific view may offer some bridges to increase our understanding. One promising idea is the fact that the human body has properties similar to that of the crystal. In his book, *Spiritual Nutrition and the Rainbow Diet,* Gabriel Cousens, M.D., states:

> "The key of understanding the assimilation of energy into our physical structure is through the awareness of our bodies as a series of synchronous, interacting crystal structures. The human body on this level is a linkage of oscillating solid and liquid crystals that form an overall energy pattern for the total body. Each organ, gland, nerve system, cell, and protein structure—even the tissue salts of the body—are a level of organization with some degree of crystalline function."[3]

Human bone, as well as the supporting voluntary muscles and the arterial tissue in the cardiovascular system, is known to have piezoelectric properties. Bone demonstrates this property by generating a measurable electromagnetic field when stressed. It appears that bone also acts as an "antenna" for receiving information, and then transmitting it to the rest of the body via its crystalline properties.[4]

The ability of bone and quartz crystal to transmit energy demonstrates their capability as semiconductors. Semiconductors are substances whose conductivity is markedly improved by the application of heat, light, or electrical current. This phenomenon occurs only in substances having a highly ordered molecular structure, as in quartz crystal. In an ordered structure, electrons can move more easily from the electron cloud surrounding one atomic nucleus to the cloud surrounding another. Randall and Vicki Baer's *The Crystal Connection,* suggests that the phenomenon of semiconduction is also apparent in the human body:

"Albert Szent-Gyorgi points out that the molecular structure of many parts of the cell is regular enough to support semiconduction.... He conjectured that protein molecules, each having a slot or station for mobile electrons, could flow in a semi-conducting current over long distances without losing energy, much as in a game of checkers where one counter would jump along a row of other pieces across the entire board."[5]

Water is also a kind of semiconductor. As a major component of the human body, it is capable of bringing ions into its structure and holding them in solution. This phenomenon is known as "structured water." When structured water in the blood organizes around an incoming micronutrient molecule, for example, it acts as a semiconductor, moving ions into the structured cytoplasmic water of the cell. Optimally, ions and molecules with free-floating electrons, such as cell salts and other minerals are attracted to the pattern created by structured water, establishing a resonance throughout the human body.

Therefore, in an imbalanced energy field there will be less structure, thereby breaking down the semiconducting properties of both water and protein. Cells are then not able to receive the ions they need.

We have given a scientific description of the crystalline properties of the human body. However, it seems that what we have said in scientific terms simply echoes these words from the Bible: "Man and woman are formed of the dust of the earth" (Genesis 2:7).

The Electromagnetic Properties of Life Force Energy and the Human Body

In order to describe our model for healing, we must now introduce another property of life force energy and the human energy system. This property is their electromagnetic nature. "In 1861-62 Baron Karl von Reichenbach, a celebrated German chemist who discovered paraffin, published a series of experiments on the odic force, or life force energy. His findings can be summarized as follows:

1. Odyle is a universal property of matter in variable and unequal distribution in both space and time.

2. It flows in concentrated form from special sources such as heat, friction, sound, electricity, light, lunar, solar and stellar rays, chemical action, and organic vital activity of living things.

3. It possesses polarity. There is negative odyle, which gives a sensation of coolness and is pleasant, and positive odyle, which gives a sensation of warmth and discomfort.

4. It can be conducted: metals, glass, resin, silk, and water all being perfect conductors...."[6]

Unfortunately, Baron von Reichenbach was largely ignored in his time, but current researchers are exploring some of his ideas, and demonstrating the electromagnetic nature of the biological system. Lakhovsky, in the *Secret Life of Plants,* states: "'The cell-organic unit in all living beings, is nothing but an electromagnetic resonator, capable of emitting and absorbing radiation of a very high frequency. These fundamental principles cover the whole field of biology."[7]

More recently, Dr. Robert Becker, in his book *The Body Electric*, describes his research in the bio-electrical potential of cells, particularly bone cells, to regenerate and heal themselves with the addition of a weak electrical current.

Dr. Randolph Stone (1890-1981) founded a modern discipline of holistic healing (polarity therapy), based on a system of mapped magnetic polarities in the body. Dr. Stone, originally trained as an osteopath and chiropractor, developed this system after years of traveling and studying healing systems all over the world. He studied both yoga and Ayurvedic medicine in India and acupuncture and herbology in the Orient. He also learned concepts of healing with life force energy taught by Paracelsus, the sixteenth century prodigy sometimes considered the first modern medical scientist.

The general idea in polarity is that if you connect a negatively charged body part with a positively charged body part, you stimulate life energy flow. A positively charged area of the body correlates with the south magnetic pole, and a negatively charged area of the body correlates with the north magnetic pole. The healing system that we will describe later in the book uses the polarity of the body to stimulate a healing energy flow, so we will describe some relevant polarities.

The back of the head is considered positive, and the base of the spine is considered negative. In Dr. Stone's system the right hand and the right side of the body have a positive polarity, and the left hand and the left side have a negative polarity. However, we have not found this to be uniformly true. By holding a pendulum over a person's hand, or by asking the person to do the exercise in the section "Familiarizing Yourself with Crystals" in Chapter 3, we have found that for some people, the right hand is negatively charged and the left hand is positively charged. This phenomenon seems somewhat related to whether a person is right-or left-handed, as well as to individual beliefs about how one gives or receives with one's hands. In our experience there has been no set pattern and the charges have had to be individually determined. But in most cases, we have found that the right hand seems to be positively charged for right-handers, and the left hand positively charged for left-handers.

In our system of healing we use the mind to visualize the flow of life force energy going from the negatively charged hand (receiving hand) to the positively charged hand (sending hand), thereby creating a directional energy flow.

Many of you may have participated in a meditation or healing circle where you were asked to hold hands and visualize receiving white healing light through your left hand and sending it to the next person through your right hand. This visualization is an example of the same principle, using the hand polarity to stimulate energy flow. It has been our experience that for those whose receiving hand is not the left hand but the right, there may be less of a sensation of energy flow in this exercise. The point to remember here is that the body consists of negatively and positively charged areas, and that you can use your mind to direct life force energy from one area to another using magnetic principles of attraction.

We have seen how interconnected our energy system is. You can work with the meridians, the subtle bodies, or with your thoughts. We have chosen to work primarily with the chakras in the book because they are relatively easy to locate and there are many simple methods of balancing them with quartz crystals. Whatever method you choose will affect the whole system.

Chapter 7

THE CHAKRAS

We have discussed the connection of the chakras to the subtle bodies of the aura. Like the aura, the chakras can be said to be a "record" of our experiences. Every chakra, when balanced, reflects a particular pattern of energy that can be sensed as a different color or perceived as a "sense perception." Using an analogy, we might say that the chakras are like windows in a house—that "house" being our body. If the windows are small or dirty, or if we close the curtains, less light can come in. In this condition, bright sunlight outside might appear as a cloudy yellow color inside the house. The degree to which the chakras are activated, balanced and able to receive life force energy depends upon our will, our belief system, and our emotional state.

We have also discussed how the chakras work to step-down life force energy into a form, which can be used by the physical body. The chakras stimulate the endocrine glands, which, in turn, secrete hormones for cell growth and maintenance as well as other bodily functions. If an endocrine gland does not receive sufficient life force energy, the system does not function properly and the result is pain or disease. Actually, pain and disease can be seen as a message that, in some way, thoughts are blocking the flow of life force energy.

When an imbalance is present in a particular chakra, the key to restoring harmony in the system lies in developing the characteristic qualities that the chakra represents. For example, if we find it difficult to express our needs, truth, or creativity, the result will be a restricted flow of energy in the throat chakra. To remedy this, we can sing. Singing can help balance the throat chakra and also uplift the spirit. By monitoring the energy flow in the chakras, we can receive accurate feedback on which of our beliefs promotes physical vitality, peace of mind, and strengthened intuitive awareness. These are the beliefs that will help connect us to the source of all life. The tones associated with the colors are the sound/color correspondences given by Col. Dinshah P. Ghadiali, who was a pioneer in color therapy who practiced in the early 1900s.[1]

Root Chakra

The root chakra has a strong affinity with our etheric body, which, in turn, is intimately connected with the gross physical body. The etheric body is linked to physical vitality, mastery of our physical bodies, and our survival sense in the physical world. When we are physically tired or stressed from physical exertion, the root chakra may feel like it needs to be charged or revitalized.

On the emotional and mental levels of our development, the root chakra expresses personal will and the desire to take action and to express ourselves in unique ways. If the root chakra is congested or deactivated, we may perceive the world as being threatening or unsafe, or we may not be able to express something that feels very basic to our individual nature.

On the spiritual level of development, the root chakra can be expressed by the following exclamation: "The universe resounds with the joyful cry, I am" (Scriabin). This is like a baby's total and spontaneous joy and delight in being. If we have deep-rooted beliefs that we don't deserve to live, that there is no place for us in the universe, or that somehow we cannot find and appreciate our uniqueness, then this may deactivate the root chakra. "Like the trees and the stars, you have a right to be here" (Desiderata).

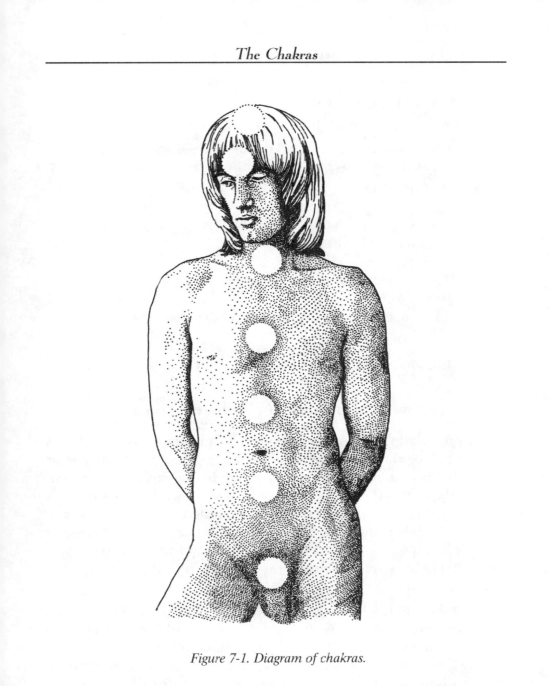

Figure 7-1. Diagram of chakras.

The color of the spectrum associated with the root chakra is red, which is an intense, focused vibration that builds vitality on the physical level and courage, perseverance, and strength on the emotional, mental, and spiritual levels.

1. Meaning: Physical vitality, basic will to be.

2. Associated color: Red.

3. Associated tone of the scale: G.

4. Endocrine glands: Gonads or adrenals—depending on the belief systems associated with our basic being.

5. Affirmations:

"I HONOR THE NATURAL PHYSICAL VITALITY OF MY BODY AND TAKE CARE OF IT WISELY."

"I AM, AND THE WORLD WELCOMES ME."

"I LIVE COURAGEOUSLY, TAKING ACTION TO EXPRESS MY BEING."

6. Location: Base of the spine, pubic bone.

Lower Abdomen or Spleen Chakra

In the traditional yogic system of chakras, the second chakra is located two or three inches below the navel. Some Western systems locate this chakra in the area of the spleen. In our experience, the energy of these two areas are definitely related, so we speak of them as one chakra. This chakra is particularly associated with the etheric and emotional subtle bodies. The first step in life is to establish our sense of being (physical/etheric level). Then we reach out and begin to connect with others and establish who we are on the feeling level of relationship (emotional level).

On the physical level of development, the lower abdomen chakra deals with assimilation and elimination (letting go). This chakra also deals with an exploration of our physical senses and of sense pleasures in the physical world. Deactivation of this chakra generally stems from overgratification of the senses. Unbalanced eating, drinking, and sexual habits often develop out of our need for security and our inability to "let go." So at the physical level we must learn moderation.

On the emotional level of development, we begin to connect with others and to seek their approval in order to validate who we are. We assimilate the impressions that others have of us and seek to understand ourselves through these "mirrored" impressions.

Sometimes deactivation of this chakra is related to holding on to old grievances and refusing to assimilate new understandings. We prefer security to change because of our sense of being "incomplete." So we attempt to fill up our emptiness by trying to take in love in the form of pleasure.

On the spiritual level of development, the lower abdomen chakra relates to the joy of being alive and to understanding the connections between all life. If we are blocked at this level of development, we may feel loneliness or basic separateness.

Many of us at times experience deactivation in the lower abdomen chakra, because we are still learning to moderate our desires and to release our desire for security. Here we are working with our desire for approval and learning how to connect with others in ways that support our uniqueness.

The lower abdomen chakra is associated with the color orange, which is a warm, expansive vibration that transmits qualities of stimulation, optimism, hope, and sociability. Orange is a good color to help banish fear and depression, and to help us reach out to others and new adventures.

1. Meaning: connecting with others through our feelings, assimilating and letting go of our experience.
2. Associated color: Orange.
3. Associated tone of the scale: A.
4. Endocrine glands: Spleen, liver, pancreas, and gonads.
5. Affirmations:

"I ASSIMILATE RIGHT UNDERSTANDING THROUGH MY FEELINGS AND SENSES."

"I WELCOME CHANGE AND FREELY LET GO OF WHAT I DON'T NEED."

"I AM ENOUGH."

"I TRUST THE UNIVERSE TO SUPPLY MY ABUNDANCE AND PROSPERITY."

6.   Location: Two inches below navel (also, lower abdominal area and spleen).

Solar Plexus Chakra

The solar plexus chakra is associated with our sense of personal identity and power and has an affinity with the emotional and mental subtle bodies. On the physical level, the solar plexus relates to learning how to both mobilize and regulate energy for conscious purposes. On the emotional and mental levels, we establish and develop who we are and learn to feel powerful in our uniqueness. Here the emphasis is on learning how to develop our self-esteem and to free ourselves from the roles we feel bound to play in life. When we are blocked at the emotional level, we may feel angry at having to work at a job that does not express who we are, or at filling others' needs without meeting our own. We may also be afraid to step forward and get what we need.

On the mental level of development, we learn to make conscious choices about what we want, and to expand whom we are through new skills and information. So our task at the solar plexus is to consciously use our mind to choose and develop a positive self-image, construct our own set of values, and establish a base of personal power.

If we are afraid to let in new ideas or hold onto old values, we may be blocked on the mental level of this chakra. If we lack confidence or a sense of power, we may sense a lack of energy here. We know that self doubts or the belief that we don't deserve the good things in life can give rise to "butterflies in the stomach." Often, in trying to deal with our emotions relating both to confidence and self-acceptance, we develop an imbalance in both the lower abdomen and solar plexus chakras. Repressed anger as well as an inability to express our personal power may deactivate both the root and solar plexus chakras.

On the spiritual level, the solar plexus chakra can be expressed as "I am unique and I walk my path with an unassuming self-assurance." This is like being in a garden and noticing the beauty of each and every flower. They are all beautiful and they are all distinct. Together, they express the manner in which diversity and uniqueness contribute to the beauty of the whole. Blockage at the spiritual level can manifest through lack of self-confidence as well as conflicts concerning whether it is "right" to believe in oneself. In the history of Christianity, and in other religious traditions, "selfishness" was considered to be a sin. Many of us still carry past-life memories from earlier Christian times and have a great deal of conflict about affirming ourselves. For us, one answer lies in observing the beauty and uniqueness of every living thing in nature.

The color associated with the solar plexus is yellow, a lighter, stimulating vibration with qualities of joy, optimism, and confidence. These are qualities we normally relate to the sun. Yellow also has the quality of helping to focus and expand the conscious, decision-making mind.

1. Meaning: Developing self-confidence and building personal power.

2. Associated color: Yellow.

3. Associated tone on the scale: A#.

4. Endocrine glands: Adrenals, liver, pancreas.

5. Affirmations:

"I OWN MY STRENGTH AND POWER."

"I APPRECIATE ALL MY WONDERFUL QUALITIES THAT MAKE ME UNIQUE."

6. Location: Two inches above the navel.

Heart Chakra

The heart chakra has an affinity with the emotional, mental, and spiritual subtle bodies. Here we learn about compassion for ourselves and others, and we experience the truth of the oneness of all creation. On the physical level, the heart chakra relates to our physical hearts as well as to blood circulation. The thymus gland, which is also located in this region, has a strong influence on our immune system.

On the emotional and mental levels of development, we must learn the importance of self-acceptance, forgiveness, and a non-judgmental attitude towards others and ourselves. Many of those who suffer heart attacks are perfectionists who may harbor anger and judgment for the mistakes of others. Lack of compassion and an overly judgmental attitude can deactivate the heart chakra, as well as the lower abdomen and solar plexus. We must learn to accept our emotions as part of our being. Our emotional responses, such as anger or fear, can often give us instant feedback on the direct consequences of our choices and decisions. Ultimately, this feedback helps us to move towards union with God/dess/all that is, rather than continuing to exist in a state of separateness. On the spiritual level, the heart chakra is associated with the understanding that we are all One—that we are connected rather than being separate from others. When someone has died or left us and we feel separate or lonely, we may deactivate the heart chakra if we try to repress the grief and sorrow. In general, we can lose energy at our heart chakra and the lower abdomen chakra as well, if we repress our feelings due to our belief that "it is weak to express feelings." Often forgiveness needs to occur at the heart, particularly self-forgiveness.

The color green is associated with the heart and it is a soothing, balancing vibration associated with harmony and compassion. I've often thought that the reason that we are surrounded by so much green in nature is to teach us about balance and compassion.

1. Meaning: Developing compassion for all, especially ourselves.

2. Associated color: Green.

3. Associated tone of the scale: C. The tone F is also associated with the heart chakra.

4. Endocrine gland: Thymus.

5. Affirmations:

"I ACCEPT MYSELF FULLY AS I AM."

"I AM TRULY LOVED."

6. Location: Heart.

Throat Chakra

The throat chakra has an affinity with the emotional, mental, and spiritual bodies—particularly the latter two. It is related to the solar plexus chakra, as both areas deal with self-expression. Emphasis at the throat is on expressing our truth and creativity and giving service to others. On the physical and emotional levels, fear of expressing something that needs to be said may create blockages resulting in sore throats and other throat problems.

On the mental level the throat chakra relates to our ability to give to others through our creativity, and the active expression of our knowledge. If we do not believe that we have something to give, or if our creative expression has been blocked, we may lose energy at the throat. Many of us have had experiences in school in which our creative expression was severely limited. Consequently, we are now learning to activate our throat chakras.

At the spiritual level of development, the throat chakra relates to service. We learn that giving to others through our uniqueness is our major function in being on the earth. It has been said that the throat chakra relates to the will. I believe that our lesson at the throat chakra is to put our will into action through service, and to make that service a creative expression of our individuality.

The color blue associated with the throat chakra brings mental peace and understanding. As blue is the color of the sky, it is also an expression of our aspirations.

1. Meaning: Speaking truth, creative expression, giving service.

2. Associated color: Blue.

3. Associated tone of the scale: D.

4. Endocrine gland: Thyroid.

5. Affirmations:

"I NOW SAY WHAT NEEDS TO BE SAID."

"I VALUE AND EXPRESS MY CREATIVITY."

"MY PURPOSE IS TO SERVE OTHERS WITH MY UNIQUE GIFTS."

6. Location: Throat.

Third Eye Chakra

While the third eye chakra is associated primarily with the spiritual subtle body, it serves a unique role as a coordinator and regulator at the physical, emotional, and mental levels of development. This chakra and the lower abdominal chakra have a complementary relationship, both focusing on our connection with life and on the processes of assimilation and elimination. On the physical level of development at the third eye chakra, the pituitary, or master gland, has a regulating function in the body. We can think of the third eye as a supervisor of our affairs, with the solar plexus often acting as the foreman, and the organs actually carrying out the orders.

On the emotional and mental levels of development, we consciously and unconsciously choose the beliefs, which determine our reality. The third eye chakra enables our beliefs to be manifested. Our subconscious mind is located here, and often our subconscious memories from childhood or past lives deactivate the third eye chakra. When we work with energy balancing, we usually put a crystal or gemstone on the third eye in order to affect the overall system. Sometimes the root of the change needs to begin here.

On the spiritual level of development, the third eye serves as a catalyst or bridge to help us connect with our higher spiritual nature. It is the seat of our intuition. As we contact and merge with the awareness of unity, we begin to receive additional impressions from beyond our five senses and everyday mind. Intuition feels like a calm sense of rightness, even when it appears in the midst of pain. Intuitive knowing comes in many forms, such as dreams, colors, symbols, sounds, pictures, feelings, sense impressions, and, quite frequently, as an ordinary thought. We can block our intuition and deactivate our third eye chakra through fear of the unknown, or our belief that knowledge can only be obtained through the rational mind and physical senses.

The color associated with the third eye is indigo, which is a deep blue tinged with violet, like the color of the twilight sky. Indigo is a very light, cooling, uplifting vibration, which has the quality of expanding spiritual understanding.

1. Meaning: Regulator and catalyst, seat of our intuitive knowing.
2. Associated color: Indigo.
3. Associated tone of the scale: D#.
4. Endocrine gland: Pituitary.

5. Affirmations:

"I NOW RELEASE EARLY LIFE AND PAST LIFE EXPERIENCES WHICH DO NOT SERVE MY HIGHEST GOOD."

"I ACCEPT RESPONSIBILITY FOR CREATING MY REALITY."

"MY INTUITIVE CONNECTION WITH MY HIGHER SPIRITUAL NATURE IS EXPANDING AND BECOMING CLEARER."

6. Location: Brow.

Crown Chakra

The crown chakra has an affinity with our spiritual subtle body. This chakra and the root chakra share a common focus on our basic sense of identity. However, at the crown we do not emphasize our individual uniqueness. Here our emphasis is on our universality, on merging with the oneness of all things. The crown is where we become One again, and merge with a sense of infinite peace and joy—the unity of all life. An imbalance at the crown chakra often means that, at that moment, we do not wish to receive guidance from our higher self. We are holding on to some belief because it is familiar, even if it is painful. Often, moving to a new level of integration involves the death of some part of us. There are times when we hold on from fear of the unknown and block the love and safety that flows into us at the crown chakra.

The color associated with the crown chakra is violet. It has a vibration that gives rise to alpha and theta brain waves. Violet also promotes the qualities of transformation and transcendence.

1. Meaning: Merging with our basic identity of God/dess/all that is.
2. Associated color: Violet.
3. Associated tone of the scale: E.
4. Endocrine gland: Pineal.

5.   Affirmations:

"I MERGE WITH THE UNITY OF ALL LIFE."

"I ACT IN ALIGNMENT WITH MY HIGHER SPIRITUAL NATURE."

6.   Location: Crown of the head.

Relationships of the Chakras

When you sense imbalances in particular chakras, you can use your understanding of their nature and function to help clear negative beliefs. You can also look for a connection between deactivated chakras. For example, if the root, heart, and throat chakras are deactivated, you can be fairly certain that something is not being expressed or communicated. In general, the quality of the energy received at the three upper chakras—the throat, brow, and crown—depends on the quality of energy at the three lower chakras: the root, lower abdomen, and solar plexus. We can improve the quality of energy flow through the chakra system by focusing unconditional love and acceptance from our hearts on any deactivated chakra. In our practice we also check the complementary pairs of chakras because they often function together:

✳   Root Chakra—Crown Chakra.
✳   Lower Abdomen Chakra—Third Eye Chakra.
✳   Solar Plexus Chakra—Throat Chakra.
✳   Heart Chakra.

Sometimes we find that working with the most deactivated chakra will help to clear and balance the entire system. When you have finished working with the chakras, it is helpful to affirm total love and unconditional acceptance in your heart. During the clearing and affirmation process you can monitor the energy flow in the chakras, and in this way receive immediate feedback on what gives optimal balance.

Chapter 8

SELF-HEALING WITH
THE 3-STEP PROCESS

The 3 Steps of Healing

Healing can be viewed as a three-step process. This involves clearing out the blocked energy that impedes growth, infusing positive healing energies, and expanding spiritual awareness through contacting the higher self.

As we have seen before, repeated negative thoughts disrupt or disorganize our energy fields, causing a restricted flow of life force energy. We often retain negative thoughts because of the subconscious belief that self-examination will only recreate the pain and perpetuate it indefinitely. This "package" of negative thoughts and feelings is then stored in our subconscious, in our subtle bodies, and in our physical body. This, in turn, manifests as an altered energy flow, making us feel "out of balance." If this blockage is not cleared, toxic wastes can build up, cells do not function optimally, and physical deterioration and disease can result.

Reprogramming our subconscious with positive, life affirming thought patterns could essentially heal the effects of negative thought patterns in the body. However, the ultimate healing solution is the act of loving and accepting oneself on the deepest level. It is possible to find the places inside ourselves that are hurting, and to give that part of us the compassion, which can heal the pain. When we can establish our own confidence, inner peace, and self-acceptance, it is possible to forgive and accept ourselves, as well as others.

When you work with others it is important to hold their perfection firmly in your mind. You must see yourself as a channel for light, unconditional love, and eternal peace. This surrounds the person with the energy of compassion, which acts as a catalyst for him or her to heal a negative thought pattern.

The first step in this model of healing is clearing. This involves becoming aware of negative thoughts, clearing them through visualization, releasing the accompanying emotions, and finally clearing the energy field itself. This is an important step because it is the mind that controls the energy flow. A moment of awareness and loving release can clear the energy field, bringing a noticeable difference in how one feels.

Once the blockages are cleared, the second step is to infuse energy into specific areas, so that the electromagnetic field is balanced and energies are flowing evenly once again. This is done with positive, affirming thoughts and visualizations, and an attitude of compassion. An example of this infusion would be visualizing an area of the body in complete balance, affirming that we are healthy, loved, and filled with vital life force energy like rivers of light. Work is also done with the electromagnetic field to infuse energy in specific areas, balance each chakra, and move energies evenly through the field.

The third step, spiritual expansion, is contacting and being receptive to the higher self through visualization and attunement. Chakras can be expanded and the electromagnetic field energies heightened for increased spiritual awareness through the use of crystal grids, which we will discuss later in this chapter.

Balancing Your Body's Energies with Crystals: Clearing

Crystals can be helpful in all three stages of attitudinal healing, and there are a number of ways you can use them to balance your body's energy field. In the method we describe here, we use our minds to direct the energy flow, and work with the magnetic polarities of our hands. We like this method because it works well with the three-step process of clearing, infusing, and expansion.

The clearing process can work to relieve pain when the pain is a sign of blockage or disruption in the energy flow. We use this process to help relieve headaches, muscle cramps, congestion, and fever, as well as bottled up fear, anger, and grief.

1. Place your receiving hand on or slightly off the painful area and get a sense of what the energy feels like. You may feel a lack of energy flow, pain, pressure, cold, heat, or discomfort in your hand.

2. Hold the crystal in your sending hand, rotating it down by your side in a counterclockwise circle. Continue rotating until you feel some pain relief or get a sense of an energy flow returning to the area. This can take anywhere from one to ten minutes. Ask your pendulum, "Do I need to continue the clearing process?" By continuing to sense what is happening in your hands and using your pendulum for feedback, you will learn to know when the energy is flowing again.

Just working with the clearing process can yield useful and even dramatic results. Here is an example of a crystal-healing incident related to us by a friend:

"My baby Alden had a fever and was listless and fussy. I received instructions on the phone from a friend who knew about crystals, and I held the crystal and my other hand the way he suggested.

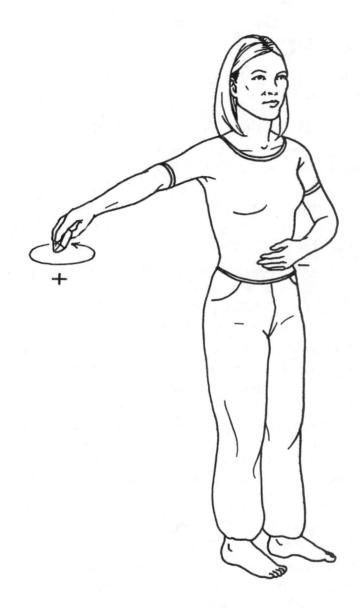

Figure 8-1. Clearing energy.

I also visualized the sick energy leaving Alden's head, going into my fingertips and out through the crystal. When it seemed enough time, the crystal stopped as if an electric current had stopped. In about five minutes Alden woke up crying, and then he settled down. The fever was gone and it didn't return."

Another woman took our crystal class and was very enthusiastic about starting to use crystals. Her opportunity came several days later when she was teaching an art class. A student of hers had come with a terrible headache and wanted to leave class. She convinced the student to lie down for a few minutes with her own left hand on her forehead and with a crystal in her right hand pointing toward the fingertips. The student felt much better in about five minutes and returned to class dumbfounded that a crystal might have helped her in some way. Our friend was elated and has continued to use crystals in innovative ways ever since.

Balancing Your Body's Energies with Crystals: Infusing

After there is an even flow of energy from the clearing process, we usually infuse or add life force energy to continue the process of healing.

1. Hold your receiving hand palm up and visualize it receiving life force energy.

2. Hold the crystal in your sending hand, pointing toward your fingertips and toward your body. Rotate the crystal clockwise over an area of your body, visualizing life force energy coming through the crystal and into your body. Continue rotating until you get a sense in your receiving hand or in your body that the area has received enough energy. (See Figure 8-2.)

Ask your pendulum, "Have I infused enough energy into this area?" Again, this can take anywhere from one to five, or even ten, minutes, although in our experience it takes less time to infuse energy than it does to get energy flowing again by clearing.

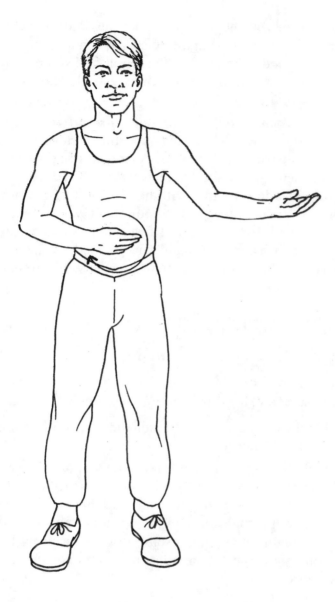

Figure 8-2. Infusing energy. Notice that the clockwise rotation is as though you are in front of your body, facing it.

Infusing energy can be particularly helpful for everyday stress and fatigue. It is also effective in building up energy in an area for long-term healing, and for creating new affirmative patterns of thought. In our experience, using the two steps together, first clearing and then infusing, brings the greatest benefit.

We visited a woman who had recently had abdominal surgery and was recuperating at home. She had been unable to breathe deeply and was too weak to get out of bed. We began with the clearing process, and the energy began to flow very quickly. We knew that what she needed, however, was a strong infusion of energy. So we placed three crystals on the bed pointing toward her body. We worked with the infusing process for about five minutes or so. She began to breathe deeply, and we worked a little more, until we felt she had taken in all the energy she could assimilate at that time. She was then able to get up and walk a few steps.

She later wrote us, saying, "Thank you for your time and effort on my behalf. I truly believe that the crystals and you two cut my healing time from intestinal surgery in half."

Our personal belief is that illness first begins with imbalanced thoughts accompanied by emotional pain. We try to help people become more aware of the imbalanced thought and to release the accompanying emotional pain. Consequently, most of our work has been with counseling rather than direct work with physical ailments. However, release of thought imbalances can sometimes have an immediate and direct physical impact.

A client with a bladder infection came to us as a last resort. She had a doctor's appointment following our session. As we talked, she began to realize how angry she was about not being able to express herself in a certain situation. We then had her lie on the healing table (fully clothed) and began to clear the bladder area, while we encouraged her to voice her anger. We then infused energy and completed the healing session. The subsequent doctor's examination showed no trace of infection.

Releasing painful past experiences and realigning our thinking takes effort and patience. Crystals can amplify the process but they are not an instant cure, and are a subtle tool that we can choose to use in our everyday life.

Balancing Your Body's Energies with Crystals: A Chakra Infusion

This is a wonderful healing meditation to do on a regular basis, in the morning to regenerate your energy instead of reaching for the coffee, or at night to help release stress and sleep more soundly.

1. Hold a mental focus such as, "I open to the unconditional love of Spirit," or "I am centered and balanced in the Divine flow."

2. Take a few deep diaphragmatic breaths before starting and during this meditation, and remain relaxed and receptive.

3. Hold the crystal in your sending hand and rotate clockwise (down and to the left) over each chakra, beginning with the root chakra, for about a half minute. Try to sense when the chakra has assimilated enough energy.

4. Hold the crystal steady, pointing toward the chakra and affirm, "I am now optimally balanced."

5. When you have finished, focus your attention on how your energy has changed, and enjoy your expanded state. This is a good preparation for further meditation.

6. End your meditation.

People in our classes who have done this exercise most often report a sense of evenness, peace, well-being, and energy renewal. I have also noticed that if I give myself a chakra infusion for two or three days before my menstrual period, uncomfortable physical symptoms are sometimes relieved.

Another variation of the infusion process works with the same hand principles as shown in the illustration (see Figure 8-3):

1. Hold the crystal in your receiving hand with the point toward the body.

2. Hold your sending hand on, or slightly off, the area of the body on which you are working. If you have two crystals then you can also have a crystal in your sending hand with the point toward your fingertips.

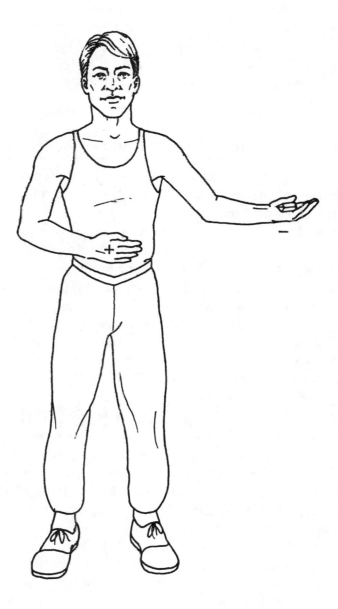

Figure 8-3. Another infusing position

You will be increasing the life force energy flow to the area as it moves from your negative receiving hand to your positive sending hand and into the body. This is a comfortable position in which to rest awhile. The process will take longer than if the sending hand is actively rotating the crystal.

Clockwise and Counterclockwise Rotation

We have observed that when you focus your intent on stimulating an energy flow for the purpose of clearing, rotating your sending hand in a counterclockwise direction seems to expedite the flow of energy. However, we have also noticed that if you focus your intent on bringing soothing relief or calm, rotating clockwise seems to feel more balancing. Therefore, the suggestion to rotate counterclockwise for clearing and clockwise for infusing is not a hard and fixed rule. We have also found that rotating clockwise for both clearing and infusing also feels balancing, particularly over the chakras. The bottom line seems to be that your perceptions are aligned with your beliefs, so that whatever movements you make with the crystal are the ones that are most compatible with your thoughts and understanding of energy.

Aligning with Your Higher Self

We have been asked, "Aren't you taking imbalanced energy into your body by this method?" There are several facets to this answer. One is that the energy flow going through your body is neutral in its effects unless you take in imbalanced energy through your thoughts and feelings. Whenever you are working with yourself or others, the idea is to move into an alignment with your higher self and the spiritual essence of the other person. When you are detached from your own emotions and thoughts, you will not assimilate imbalanced vibrations. However, I have been aware of experiencing imbalanced energies in my own body when someone is working on an issue that is relevant for me. Suggestions are to:

✳ Affirm that you are One with the unconditional love of Spirit, and continue to hold that focus during the healing session.

✳ Visualize yourself surrounded and infused by White Light during the session.

✳ Take time after your session to clear and infuse your own energies.

Becoming more aware of how you are affected by the healing process of someone else can give you increased insight about your own healing process.

Spiritual Expansion with Crystal Grids

In addition to working actively with the energy field, it is also possible to create a healing energy field with crystals that serves as a template or perfect healing form. You can create powerful, spiritually expansive energy fields by making geometric patterns with crystals that we call crystal grids. A grid maintains a steady flow of energy that merges with your human energy field as you sit or lie receptively within its form. Merging with the spiritual qualities of shapes aligns you with your higher self, planet Earth, and the greater macrocosm of spiritual reality.

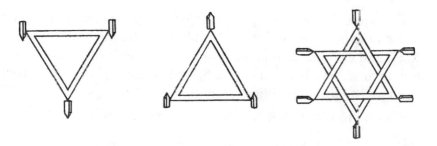

Figure 8-4. Inverted triangle, upright triangle, and Star of David.

The mineral kingdom resonates especially well with the numbers three, four, and six (and 12 as a multiple of three, four, and six). Molecules and groups of molecules that bond together in triangles, squares, and hexagons leave no space and therefore they conserve energy. Five does not appear in the mineral kingdom because five sided polygons do not pack tightly together without any spaces in between, as do triangles, squares, and hexagons.

The triangle symbolizes spiritual synthesis, and is the completion of the conflict presented by dualism. It resonates with mental energy, because it is the mental mind that seeks experience and learns from it. We assimilate and synthesize from our experiences and build our beliefs based on those experiences. The "three principle" expressed to its highest potential shows spirit and matter united by the mind.

The triangle also resonates to the element of Fire, and one facet of Fire is expressing your highest potential through the act of creating. The energy of Fire is a harmonious flow.

Affirmations that you can use with a crystal triangle are:

"I THINK CLEARLY, SYNTHESIZING INFORMATION FROM ALL LEVELS OF MY BEING."

"I CREATE BALANCE BY CENTERING MY ATTENTION ON WHAT I AM CREATING IN THE PRESENT MOMENT."

"WHEN MY PERSONAL WILL IS ALIGNED WITH DIVINE WILL, THE ENERGY OF CREATION FLOWS EFFORTLESSLY."

The square represents the uniting of heart and mind toward the manifestation of spirit on Earth. It symbolizes the qualities of patience, stability, and endurance that we develop as a result of focusing our intent in a particular direction over a period of time. The square grounds you and assists you in building strength.

Affirmations that you can use with a crystal square are:

"MY VISION IS TO MANIFEST SPIRIT IN PHYSICAL FORM."

"THE EARTH GROUNDS AND NOURISHES ME."

"I CULTIVATE PATIENCE, HONORING THE TIME IT TAKES ME TO GROW IN SPIRITUAL WISDOM."

"I AM CENTERED IN THE SECURITY AND ABUNDANCE OF MY OWN POWER."

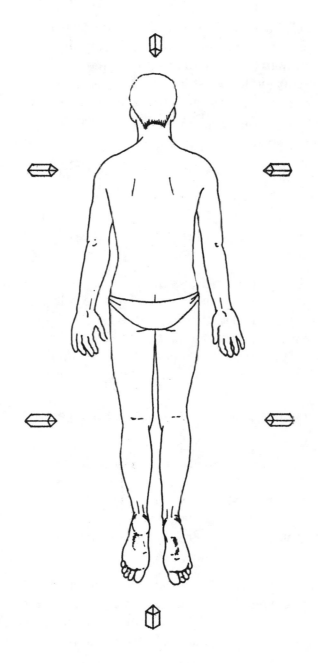

Figure 8-5. Star of David crystal grid.

The Star of David is a powerful form to use because of the hexagonal shape of the crystal. It symbolizes giving and receiving unconditional love through compassion toward self and other. It is also associated with the practical idealism of service. The "six principle" can assist you in manifesting union, harmony, equilibrium, and grace. A phrase often associated with the Star of David is, "As above, so below."

Affirmations that you can use with the Star of David are:

"THE GRACE OF UNCONDITIONAL LOVE IS MY BIRTHRIGHT."

"JOY LIGHTS MY WAY, AND I SHARE THAT JOY WITH OTHERS."

"I MANIFEST SPIRIT ON EARTH THROUGH GIVING AND RECEIVING UNCONDITIONAL LOVE."

The "five principle" is common in plants and animals, where it allows for diversity in form. Its meanings are relevant to the spiritual expansion process, and so the five pointed star is a useful grid to create. The five-pointed star represents the knowledge that we gain through seeking new experiences in order to grow. It stimulates our movement towards the unknown, where we seek to break through our limitations in order to change and expand.

Affirmations that you can use with a five-pointed star are:

"I AM NOW FREE, INDEPENDENT, AND CREATIVE, AS I EXPAND BEYOND PERCEIVED LIMITATIONS FROM MY PAST."

"I ALIGN MY PERSONAL WILL WITH DIVINE WILL."

"I LOOK FOR THE GROWTH OPPORTUNITIES THAT THE CHANGES IN MY LIFE ARE BRINGING ME."

If you have 12 crystals, you can make a circle that looks like a clock face. The circle symbolizes the unified energy of wholeness, and the state of "being" rather than "doing." It assists you in accepting yourself as you are in each moment. It is energy of renewal and new beginnings.

Affirmations that you can use with the circle are:

"I MERGE WITH THE PEACE AND STILLNESS OF THE ETERNAL PRESENT."

"I MOVE BEYOND PERSONAL IDENTITY INTO GREATER ONENESS WITH ALL LIFE."

For meditation, you can make a crystal grid, in which you can sit or lie. Start with the points facing in toward you. This pattern will assist you in moving into an altered state, and it will recharge your energy field. If your intention is sending your light to others or the planet, you can turn the crystals so that the points face out. Crystals clusters can also be used for a more diffuse field. They heighten the positive energies in a space where you are working with healing.

You can make a circle with 12 crystals pointed in a clockwise direction. This pattern can assist you in attuning to the spiritual energies that are present with you. We experience it as stabilizing and strengthening.

The circle made with the crystals pointing counterclockwise opens you to change and transformation. We experience it as expansive, dynamic, and helpful for breaking through limiting beliefs.

We give a meditation in Chapter 9 for spiritual expansion using the grids. We all have a great deal to learn about sacred forms and patterns as healing tools, and crystals will play an important role in amplifying these forms of energy in the future.

Some Comments on the Transformation Process

People process energy in different ways. During a practice, you may experience spontaneous jerking or twitches as energy changes occur. Parts of your body may tingle, or get hot or cold. You may receive vivid imagery of energy movements. More commonly, you may utilize energy more gradually and not notice anything happening except that you feel more relaxed.

In attempting to use crystals for physical healing, we have noticed that sometimes we get relief from discomfort, and sometimes nothing seems to happen. Often there is slow progress, and sometimes nothing seems to work. We believe a key factor is the intensity of the emotions and beliefs involved. For example, I have gotten muscle cramps from sleeping in a position that stresses the muscles. Crystal balancing has eased the pain with this primarily physical problem. I have also tried crystal balancing for a sore throat, and it gets better but not without some processing about why my immune system is compromised, more than one energy session, plus a lot of herbs and vitamins. The point here is not to judge yourself if nothing seems to happen.

The growth process needs to be viewed as an ongoing experience, and you need to release your attachment to particular outcomes, and seeing results within a certain time frame. Beliefs and attitudes that have existed for a long time require patience and persistence to change. The setbacks that you experience require compassion and self-acceptance. The purpose of challenges is to help you build the soul qualities of unconditional love and wisdom. Over time you will notice that you are able to respond differently in situations that once caused you pain and your self-esteem will strengthen. The key is to honor each step of the process, and to trust that Spirit is supporting you.

Chapter 9

MORE SELF-HEALING TECHNIQUES

I n this chapter we will illustrate how you can work with crystals using the three-step process for your overall well-being. We will also discuss some other possibilities for healing which you may try. The ideas included here and in the rest of the book are ones we have tried and found to be effective. Above all, it is important for you to find your own ways of working with crystals. Let these ideas be "seed thoughts" to get you started and to excite you into further exploration.

You can work with your thoughts using programmed crystals, or you can work on your energy field with healing crystals. Sometimes you will do a combination of both.

Attitudinal Healing with the 3 Steps

Clearing

1. You can sit in a crystal grid, using the pattern to amplify your mental work. If you have three crystals, place one behind you, and one at each knee. All three points face outward. If you have six crystals, make a Star of David with the points facing out.

2. Hold a crystal in your receiving hand with the point towards the body. You can program this crystal to bring up and release negative energy. You can also program it with the kind of music that has a soothing and cathartic effect on you. If you program a crystal to remember your dreams, it can also help you become aware of what needs to be cleared from your subconscious.

3. You can use the following visualization to contact your subconscious and to increase your awareness of what needs to be cleared:

GO TO YOUR FAVORITE BEAUTIFUL OUTDOOR PLACE. IT IS A BEAUTIFUL SUNNY DAY WITH PUFFY CLOUDS FLOATING BY. THE SUN IS WARM ON YOUR FACE AND THE BREEZE IS PLEASANT AND SOOTHING. OBSERVE THIS PLACE WITH ALL YOUR SENSES AND FEEL THE SAFETY AND PEACE THAT IS HERE FOR YOU. FIND A NATURAL OBJECT HERE THAT APPEALS TO YOU. BECOME TINY AND ENTER IT, EXPLORING ITS TEXTURES, FRAGRANCES, AND SOUNDS. WHILE YOU ARE HERE ASK YOUR SUBCONSCIOUS TO GIVE YOU A VISUAL PICTURE, SENSE IMPRESSION, SYMBOL, OR FEELING ABOUT WHAT NEEDS TO BE RELEASED. ASK FROM WHAT AREA OF THE BODY THE CLEARING NEEDS TO TAKE PLACE. ASK ANY OTHER PARTS OF YOUR BODY TO SPEAK TO YOU. WAIT RECEPTIVELY AND OPENLY, KNOWING THAT YOU ARE TOTALLY SAFE. WHEN YOU HAVE RECEIVED YOUR MESSAGE, COME OUT OF THE NATURAL OBJECT AND SIT ONCE AGAIN IN YOUR BEAUTIFUL PLACE. VISUALIZE THE VIOLET FLAME OF PURIFICATION OR STREAMS OF WATER OR LIGHT CLEANSING AND PURIFYING YOU. INFUSE THE ELEMENT YOU HAVE CHOSEN TO RELEASE WITH AN AFFIRMING QUALITY SUCH AS PATIENCE OR COMPASSION. LET GO.

Infusing

1. Sit in a crystal grid described earlier in this chapter, with the points facing towards you.

2. Hold a special programmed crystal in your receiving hand with the point toward the body. The crystal can be programmed for self-empowerment, optimal health, or other qualities you wish to affirm.

3. Here is an affirmative visualization you can use:

ONCE AGAIN, SEE YOURSELF IN A BEAUTIFUL PLACE. BREATHE IN THE FRAGRANT AIR. NOTICE THE TEXTURES OF THE AREA YOU ARE STANDING OR SITTING IN. LISTEN TO THE SOUNDS. GRADUALLY, YOU BECOME RELAXED AND STILL IN THE PEACEFULNESS OF THIS PLACE. CALL YOUR HIGHER SELF TO BE WITH YOU AND NOTICE THE ENERGY CHANGES. YOU ARE SURROUNDED WITH A ROSY GOLDEN LIGHT OF SAFETY AND UNCONDITIONAL LOVE. FEEL THE TOTAL ACCEPTANCE YOUR HIGHER SELF GIVES YOU. SEE YOURSELF SURROUNDED BY LOVING FRIENDS. LOOK INTO THE EYES OF EACH ONE. SEE HOW THEY DELIGHT IN YOU. HEAR THEIR WORDS OF APPRECIATION. IN THE CIRCLE OF THEIR LOVE VISUALIZE YOURSELF BEING AND ACTING THE WAY YOU WISH TO BE. AS EACH FRIEND TURNS TO LEAVE, HE OR SHE GIVES YOU A GIFT, A SYMBOL OF YOUR STRENGTH. WHEN YOU ARE READY TO LEAVE YOUR BEAUTIFUL PLACE, KNOW THAT YOUR HIGHER SELF IS ALWAYS WITH YOU AND THAT YOU ARE A PRECIOUS FLOWER, A DELIGHT IN THE WORLD, AND MUCH LOVED AND APPRECIATED.

Spiritual Expansion

1. Sit or lie in a crystal grid with the points facing in toward you. In this example we will use the five-pointed star.

2. The geometric pattern you have created is a form of light. Visualize the five-pointed star and imagine that you are one with it.

3. Focus your attention on your physical body. Open your physical body to receive the energy of the five-pointed star, and be aware of your physical energy. Notice how you respond.

4. Open your heart and imagine the colors of the five-pointed star. Ask your higher self what you can do to sustain your emotional balance.

5. Focus your awareness on your mental mind, and be receptive to the qualities of the five-pointed star. How does your mental mind change? Ask your higher self for guidance concerning your life.

6. Focus on your breathing, and detach from your emotional/mental mind. Remain in a relaxed state and be aware of any intuitive impressions that you receive.

7. Gradually reconnect with your mind, emotions, and physical body.

8. Thank the crystals and the geometric form of light for their service to you, and end the meditation. Open your eyes, feeling balanced and revitalized.

* * *

In practice, this three-step healing process flows and blends together, and you can move back and forth, releasing, affirming, and seeking higher guidance. We examine the steps mainly to illustrate and clarify how crystals can be used to amplify the process.

Laying Crystals on Your Body: Chakra Meditations

A simple method of balancing the energy field is to follow the steps for clearing and chakra infusion given in the last chapter, using a crystal programmed for optimal well-being at all levels. This is an easy practice because it requires only one crystal.

However, we have found that a set of seven personal chakra crystals, each programmed for a specific chakra, can be very beneficial. We label our crystals to insure that the same crystal is always placed on the same chakra. You can program these crystals with chakra affirmations, color, or sound, according to your perceptions about the chakras. You place the crystals on the chakras according to your intent. (See Figure 9-1.) Here are two simple meditations for clearing:

1. Place your chakra crystals on their respective chakras, pointing toward the feet.

2. If you wish to have a crystal in your hand, you can hold it in your sending hand with the point toward the fingertips.

3. In your mind, send the imbalanced energy into the core of the Earth and ask that it be purified. Hold this focus until you feel a greater sense of balance.

4. Ask for the energy of the Earth to support you and remain in a receptive state of a deeper relationship with the Earth.

5. Thank the Earth and the crystals for their help in balancing your energies, and end your meditation.

In this next meditation the directional system works effectively although it feels a little different:

1. Place chakra crystals on the solar plexus, lower abdomen, and root chakras, pointing toward the feet.

2. Put chakra crystals on the heart, throat, third eye, and crown pointing up toward the head. (In the case of the crown chakra this means pointing up above the head.)

3. You can use the image of a violet flame transforming the imbalanced energy at each chakra until it feels clear.

4. Remain for a few minutes in a state of peace and oneness.

5. Thank your crystals and your higher self for their assistance, and end your meditation.

A basic way to balance your energies is the following meditation:

1. Place your chakra crystals on your body pointing upward toward your head.

2. Begin with the root chakra and visualize white light at this chakra. You may find that the color is muddy, or cloudy. Hold the focus of optimal balance, until the light is bright and you have a sense that the chakra has received enough energy.

3. Continue with each chakra.

4. Remain in a receptive state of oneness.

5. Thank your crystals and your higher self for their assistance, and end your meditation.

For spiritual expansion, you can make a Star of David grid of crystals at your crown, with the points facing out. (See Figure 9-2).

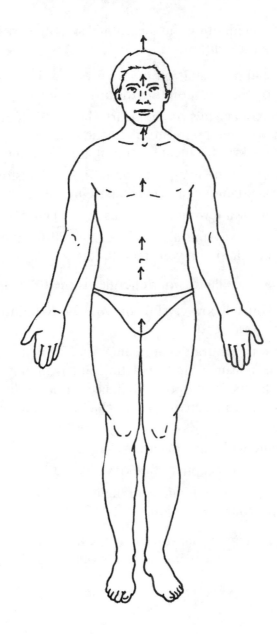

Figure 9-1. Chakra crystal layout.

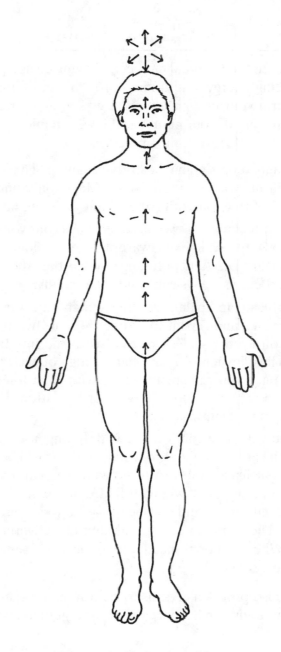

Figure 9-2. Chakra crystal layout.

Crystals and Toning

Since ancient times, sound has been recognized as a powerful healing and balancing energy, and toning through a crystal is a wonderful way to transform your energies. Hold a crystal in your sending hand, pointing out, in front of your mouth as if it were a microphone, which it is. Here are some effective toning practices:

1. Sigh, and keep sighing. Also try groaning. This works well for clearing your emotional body. Make tones until you feel a sense of freedom, of lightness, and of being unburdened.

2. Another technique for clearing is to use your voice to go up and down the scale like a warning siren, as high and low as you can go. This kind of toning also has the effect of freeing blocked energy, physically and emotionally.

3. For infusing and balancing, buy a pitch pipe. Give yourself the tone C, and repeat that tone three to five times. Continue on up the scale. Try to discern the intuitive signals that tell you when you have had enough of each tone. With experience you will spend longer with each tone, and you will know when to stop. The first step is to attune with sound, which comes with practice.

4. As you get more comfortable with toning, ask your higher guidance for a tone that you need, and you will be guided to make particular tones. Alternatively, you can try different tones, and one tone will feel right. For me, my body drinks in the right tone, and "pushes away" a tone that it doesn't need. The right tone is stimulating or activating in some way. When you don't need a tone there is a sense of nothing happening.

You can also program crystals with a tuning fork, and place them on areas of the body for healing. Follow the guidelines for programming crystals.

Quick Energizing

As we have seen earlier, vital life force energies enter into the chakras. Life force energies also enter through the feet and hands, and through the head, at the base of the skull and at the crown. You can place crystals on these areas to infuse energies (see following illustrations). Use whatever number of crystals you have, using the illustrations as suggestions.

Crystal Water

Our body is almost 70 percent water. The more structured the water in our body becomes, the more it can act as an effective semiconductor for life force energy. Drinking crystal water is an effective way to optimize our bodily functioning. You can make crystal water by placing a crystal in a glass container, and adding spring water that you can purchase from a grocery store. Set it in the sun for a minimum of six hours or so. We use a gallon jar that restaurants use for mayonnaise and pickles. You can try an experiment: hold your pendulum over a glass of tap water and ask to be shown the strength of the life force energy in the water. Then hold your pendulum over a glass of crystal water, asking the same question. The crystal water will probably have more life force energy. You can use your pendulum to determine how many glasses to drink each day and whether the water should be taken with herbs, homeopathic remedies, etc. Generally we drink crystal water instead of regular drinking water, and we do not take it with other remedies or medications. Heating or cooling crystal water affects the life force energy so keep it at room temperature. You can program the crystals you use to make crystal water for optimal health at all levels.

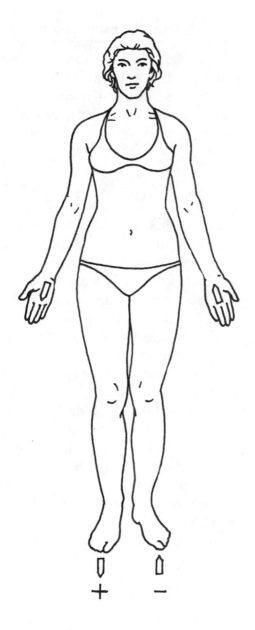

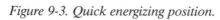

Figure 9-3. Quick energizing position.

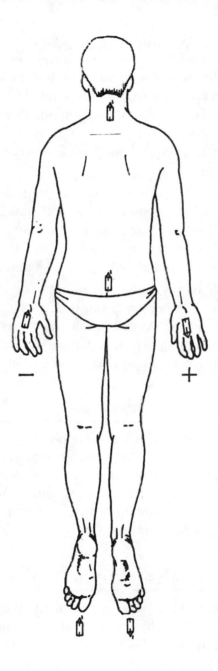

Figure 9-4. Quick energizing position.

Wearing a Crystal

You can amplify your own body's energies by wearing or carrying a single-pointed or doubly terminated crystal. The crystal helps stabilize and balance physical and emotional ups and downs, and helps transform any negative energy coming in. You can visualize yourself as "protected inside a large crystal and bathed in crystal light."

A pendant will stimulate and balance your energies in whatever direction the point is facing. Worn with the point down over the heart, it can ground your energies, stimulate your thymus gland, and amplify your compassion. With the point up, your spiritual growth can be expanded. A doubly terminated crystal accomplishes both tasks. A crystal work at the throat will stimulate your thyroid gland and your creativity.

Our experience has been that a pendant or crystal that you wear or carry on a daily basis can become saturated, although it will still retain its symbolic value for you. As our sensitivity to crystals increased, we found ourselves cleaning the crystals that we wore daily. Listen to your intuition because everyone's needs and perceptions are different.

Dreams

A crystal can be placed under your pillow, point up, to help you remember your dreams. You may remember more details and the impressions may be more vivid. Double-terminated crystals are nice for this purpose, and you maybe able to tape a small one to your third eye. We cleaned ours daily, and you must watch for saturation, because they do a lot of balancing while you sleep.

Overstimulation

Part of your learning process is identifying the intuitive messages that your body has had all the energy that it can integrate at this particular time. One way to do this is to place a crystal on a chakra or an imbalanced area of your body. Ask your pendulum to show you by making a "no" movement, when you have received enough energy. Pay attention to the energy sensations in your body.

You can also ask your body directly to show you what too much energy feels like for you, and watch for any feelings of discomfort, or a jittery feeling. Another sign of too much energy is feeling discordant or erratic, rather than centered or balanced.

If you feel these symptoms, lay your crystals aside, and give yourself time to assimilate the life force energies. Use your pendulum to ask when and how to resume your crystal meditations. No two people are alike in these matters, and your beliefs about the process, growth, and healing all influence how your body reacts. Experiment and observe yourself carefully, and you will find the best ways to keep your energy at optimal levels.

Chapter 10

CRYSTAL HEALING
WITH OTHERS

When working with others it is important to understand that you are primarily a catalyst or helper, for in the end we heal ourselves. You can enhance the optimal flow of energy in another person, but remember that the energy flow is controlled by the thoughts coming from the subconscious, conscious, and super-conscious levels. The client gains a greater sense of his power to control the attitudes necessary for healing by participating in his or her own healing through visualizations and other intuitive processes. This participation also tunes one back into one's own intuition for guidance. The healer facilitates the energy flow and assists this process by providing a safe and nurturing environment of crystal energy and healing thoughts.

In this chapter we will discuss a few simple ways that you can work with others, in addition to the ideas previously mentioned. The ideas on self-healing in Chapter 9 can also apply to working on healing others. However, it is a good idea to first become familiar with crystal energy by working on yourself. We will then describe a step-by-step energy balancing process that you can do with one to five crystals, depending on your preference. In all crystal healing work the client can be fully clothed, because crystal energies can be transmitted through clothing. If you decide to work otherwise, it is a matter of your own personal preference.

Sending Energy Through Your Hands

Crystals placed on specific areas of the body or on the chakras are among the most common ways of using crystals for healing. Use your intuition to sense where to place the crystals. When you are first learning, place the crystal on any sore or tense spot.

The crystal amplifies the life force energy of the breath. You can utilize this energy of the breath for healing and also for moving into deeper altered states. Try this simple but effective meditation:

1. Place a crystal on a part of your body that is tense or needs healing.

2. Ask for the following energies to be with you, and try to sense to presence of each one. For example:

   "I ASK FOR THE SPIRITUAL CONSCIOUSNESS OF THE CRYSTAL TO BE WITH ME." (PAUSE.)

   "I ASK FOR MY HIGHER SELF TO BE WITH ME AT THIS TIME." (PAUSE.)

   "I ASK FOR THE ANGELIC PRESENCES THAT ARE ASSISTING ME IN MY HEALING TO BE WITH ME." (PAUSE.)

3. Take a few deep diaphragmatic breaths, listening to the sound of your breath, or sensing the rise and fall of your chest and abdomen. Allow yourself to relax into an altered state.

4. Inhale, taking short, sharp breaths and contracting your abdominal muscles. Imagine that you are inhaling the unconditional love of white light. Breathing in this manner intensifies the power of this thought.

5. Upon exhaling, bathe this part of your body with light, and imagine that the crystal is aiding you in restoring balance to this area. Relax your body on this exhale.

6. Keep up this breathing rhythm until you have a sense that your body has taken in as much as it can integrate at this time.

7. Remain receptive and open, and become aware of the changes in your body. You may notice a greater relaxation in the area, changes in your breathing, less discomfort, or more emotional peace.

8. Thank your higher self, the spiritual consciousness of the crystal, and the angelic presences for their help and end your meditation.

9. Clean your crystal.

This is powerful meditation without the crystal, and the crystal serves to amplify the energy sensations so that you can perceive them more easily. It also supports the energetic balancing process. Keep in mind however that healing involves changing your thoughts. An energetic state of balance offers you the opportunities to perceive things differently and to change your beliefs toward a greater sense of self-worth, as you merge with all that is.

Steps for a Healing Session

Crystals Used

It is helpful to have the following crystals when you begin to do crystal healing work:

1. A crystal that is programmed for optimal well-being at all levels which you hold in your sending hand. It is wise to include the protection phrase "without absorbing imbalanced energies." In the energy balancing session described below, we will call this the hand-held crystal.

2. A programmed crystal for the base of the spine. This crystal plays a role in realigning the positive-negative balance at the base of the spine, and amplifies the life force energy present there.

3. Crystals for the hands. The receiving hand crystal can be programmed for receiving unconditional love, optimal energy for well-being, or intuitive guidance. The sending hand crystal can be programmed to release imbalanced energy through the sending hand, while amplifying the energy flow.

4. A crystal for the base of the skull. This is the "basic brain" area, which receives energy and sends it to different parts of the body—a "circuit dispatcher area." The crystal can be programmed to receive and amplify life-giving energy.

Preparation for Healing

Take five minutes or so for the following preparations:

1. Drink crystal water.

2. Center yourself and affirm that your work is for the highest good of the client. Focus on the positive, uplifting qualities of that person, seeing them in the perfection of the light.

3. Welcome guides and healing beings of light to work with you and through you for healing.

4. Attune to the Star of David, visualizing the client in that grid.

5. Affirm that no imbalanced energies will be absorbed, as you visualize yourself surrounded by white light.

6. Affirm that the energy to be cleared from the person is being transmuted and transformed.

7. Attune yourself with your healing crystal.

Preparation for the Client

1. Drink crystal water.

2. Check to determine client's sending and receiving hand.

Working on the Back

Step One—Clearing on the back

1. The client lies on his or her stomach. Ask the client to visualize a shower of light, relaxing and purifying the body. This process can clear away some "static electricity." opening the way for greater conscious effort. The client can also practice relaxing specific parts of the back.

2. Place a crystal in the sending hand, pointing toward the fingertips.

3. Scan the back and legs with your sensing hand, about four inches from the body, for areas of blocked energy. Often, there will be blockages in the area of the adrenal glands and shoulders.

4. Roll the crystal, pointing down between your hands, over the back, to begin clearing.

5. Continue to clear blocked areas by placing your receiving hand over the area and rotating your sending hand with the crystal counterclockwise, down at your side. (This is the clearing position first described in Chapter 8.) In general, we work from the base of the spine, over both adrenals, up the back, and across the shoulders. Then we check the neck and head. If the client is using the clearing shower of light visualization, you may want to work in the direction from the head to the feet.

6. Check the energy flow in the buttocks and legs and do any clearing needed there until all clearing is completed and you can feel the energy flowing again. Often, working in one or two trouble spots, like the adrenals, will clear the energy in the back.

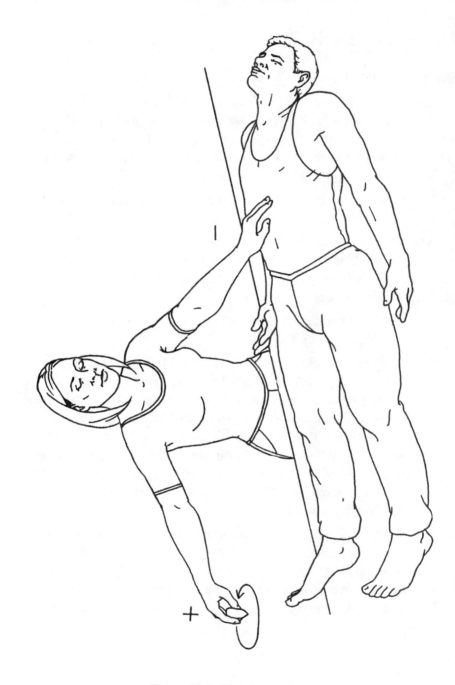

Figure 10-1. Clearing energy.

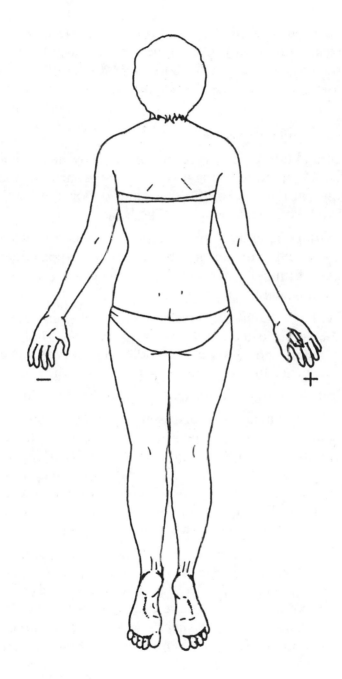

Figure 10-2. Clearing on the back.

7. Ask your pendulum to confirm that you have done all the clearing necessary at this time. You can also hold the pendulum over areas of the back and look for a "yes" answer, asking, "Is this area adequately cleared?"

Step Two—Infusing on the back

1. In addition to the crystal in the sending hand, place one crystal in the receiving hand pointing toward the body, and one on the base of the spine and one at the base of the skull, both pointing toward the head.

2. During the infusion process the client can visualize energy and strength revitalizing the body. Other appropriate healing affirmations may be used, or the client may simply remain receptive and relaxed.

3. With your hand-held crystal, infuse energy into the base of the spine, using clockwise rotations, and then into the adrenals, shoulders, and any other areas where you cleared blockages. Infuse energy over the base of the skull.

4. Infuse energy into the buttocks and legs as needed.

5. After scanning with your sensing hand, check with your pendulum to see if the major areas have received the optimal amount of energy needed at this time. Working with the pendulum will help you fine-tune your perception of energy sensations until the time comes when you don't need to use it. When you are first beginning, it can help build your confidence about what you are sensing.

6. Finish evening the flow of energy in the back by making several large, circular passes around and above the body, with your hand-held crystal pointing toward the body. Move in the direction of the energy circuit in the hands. If the right hand is the receiving hand, move in a counterclockwise rotation. If the left hand is the receiving hand, move in a clockwise rotation.

7. Remove the crystals from the back and receiving hand and ask the client to turn over.

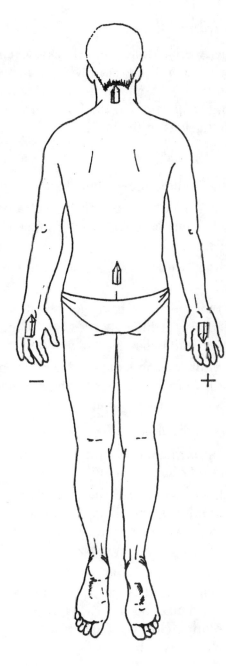

Figure 10-3. Infusing on the back.

Working on the Front

When extensive work is done on the back, there is sometimes much less work to be done on the front. However, some people process more easily lying on their back, so sometimes we work on the front only. It is possible to do energy balancing on the front only, but it is not as thorough as work on both sides of the body.

Step One—Clearing on the front

1. The client is holding the sending hand crystal.

2. Ask the client to dialogue with the subconscious self and find out what needs releasing, and then visualize the release process occurring.

3. Scan the body with your sensing hand as you did on the back for blocked areas.

4. Clear any blocked areas, using your hand-held crystal, until you feel the flow being restored. Check the legs after you have checked and balanced the chakras.

5. Scan with your sensing hand to check for energy flow, and confirm with your pendulum that the optimal level of clearing for this time has been done.

Step Two—Infusing on the front

1. Put a crystal in the client's receiving hand, in addition to the crystal in the sending hand.

2. Ask the client to visualize white light or qualities such as courage and joy. Or the client can work with affirmations, which resonate with his or her intuitive guidance. Most of all, the client can focus on self-acceptance.

3. Infuse energy with your hand-held crystal, first in the chakras where you cleared blockages, and then in any other areas where you worked. You can also work systematically up the chakras, rotating clockwise. Confirm with your pendulum that each chakra is in balance.

4. You may choose to rotate clockwise over each leg, beginning at the foot and working up the leg, checking for optimal energy flow.

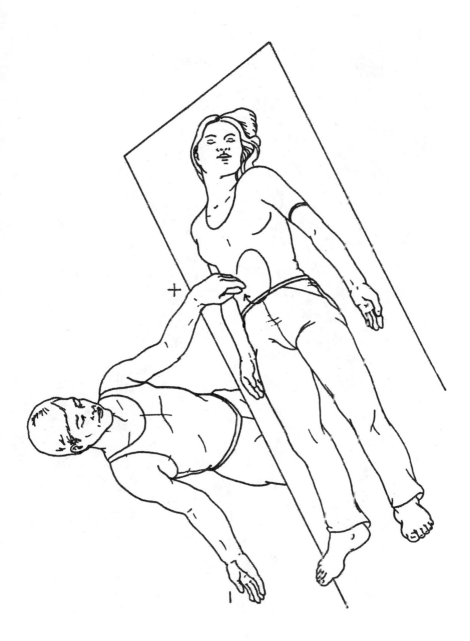

Figure 10-4. Infusing energy.

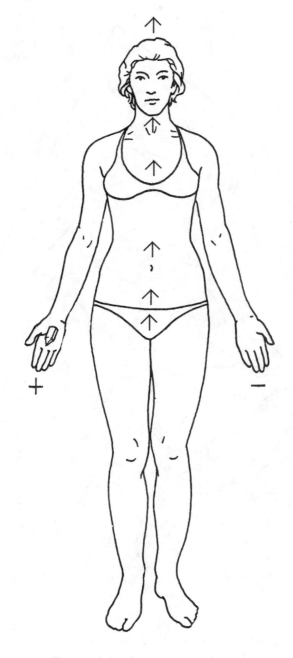

Figure 10-5. Clearing on the front.

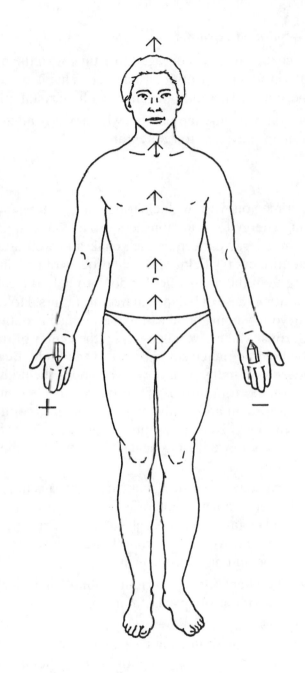

Figure 10-6. Infusing on the front.

Step Three—Spiritual expansion on the front

1. The client can be encouraged to attune with the higher self while in a state of optimal balance. This is a particularly good time to surround the client with a crystal grid.

2. You can conclude the process with any affirming thoughts that help the client to reintegrate.

Completion

1. Any time you work with clearing energy imbalances or infusing energy for consciousness expansion, you are changing the energy pattern at each chakra as well as activating the entire energy field. The final process of evening out the energies in the energy field is done to help the client function with a sense of balance in worldly affairs. Hold the crystal in your sending hand with the point facing out from your fingertips. Make several passes up the center of the client's body holding the crystal parallel to the body. Begin at the highest level that you have worked above the body, moving from the bottom of the feet to the head. Then move to a level approximately halfway between that point and the physical body. Repeat the process in the etheric body several inches above the physical body to balance the energies on that level.

2. The next step is to affirm that each chakra is now at its optimal level of functioning for grounding and balance. Have the client begin at the crown chakra and affirm optimal functioning, while you point your hand-held crystal at each chakra, beginning with the crown chakra.

3. Give the client time to reorient while lying on the table. Have him or her sit upright for a moment before getting off the table.

4. If the client is still feeling dizzy, have him or her stand up while you do a standing chakra balance. Sometimes dizziness occurs if the client goes out of the body during a session and re-enters the body too quickly. Here are the steps for a standing chakra balance:

a. Stand at the side of the client with the crystal in your sending hand.

b. Place your receiving hand over the base of the spine and your sending hand over the root chakra. (The client is standing between your hands.)

c. Visualize an energy flow going from your sending hand, through your client, to your receiving hand.

d. Move your hands together slowly up the body. The crystal will be pointing at each chakra in turn.

e. At the crown chakra, touch the crystal to your receiving hand and hold the crystal pointed up above the crown.

f. Move your receiving hand down along the back, to the base of the spine, and gently remove your hands.

5. Encourage the client to go outdoors and take a walk or stand against a tree. Physical contact with the earth is very beneficial for the body.

6. Give the client crystal water to drink. This practice helps maintain the new level of energy.

7. Wash your hands and visualize a waterfall cleansing, purifying, and filling you with light and love. Appreciate your sense of oneness with all.

8. Work with a visualization that clears the room or use some sage smoke. Clean and charge your crystals.

The Crystal Pendulum as a Healing Tool

A crystal pendulum works well to infuse color, sound, or energy into a chakra. It is best to use a crystal pendulum specifically programmed for healing rather than a pendulum used for higher guidance. Be certain that it has been cleaned and charged. You may have already noticed that when you first hold a crystal it feels very active, as it is releasing energy to balance with your system. Then, the crystal seems to become "quieter." In the same way, the pendulum responds through movement to correct an imbalance, becoming still when balance has been restored.

Hold the pendulum in your sending hand, three or four inches over each chakra, beginning with the root chakra. If you wish, you can hold a crystal in your receiving hand, pointing toward your body, to amplify the energy flow. If the pendulum rotates, the area needs energy. Continue to hold the rotating pendulum over the chakra until it becomes still. It may rotate either clockwise or counterclockwise, although one way will usually predominate. Affirm that the chakra is receiving what it needs.

If you wish to work with color, you can use a slide projector, focusing each color of the spectrum on its respective chakra. Begin with red on the root chakra. It is fascinating to watch each chakra take in varying amounts of color. Color from a slide projector affects mostly the etheric subtle body, so you can hold the pendulum about an inch and a half, to two inches above the body. It takes us about twenty to thirty minutes to balance energies with color and a crystal pendulum.

You can use the crystal pendulum for absentee healing, using a picture or an image from your mind. You can infuse the energy into a person's energy field with the following process: Begin sending healing energy to the person in your thoughts. The pendulum will probably start rotating to bring optimal balance. If the pendulum doesn't start to rotate, you can initiate a clockwise rotation. Continue sending energy until the pendulum becomes still. Then the session is complete.

There are many ways you can expand your work with the pendulum, and we hope we have stimulated your exploration in this area. The most important thing to remember is to remain centered and relaxed, learning to sense when you may be influencing the results. In this way you become more in harmony with your higher will.

Clearing the Environment

An important idea to consider is our responsibility in clearing the healing environment. First, we can sensitize ourselves to our healing room so that we know when the energies need to be purified. It is also important to acknowledge our co-creative relationship with the devas and other spiritual beings in transforming our environment. It is part of our learning as humans to take responsibility for our actions.

1. Work with your thoughts to transform energy. First, acknowledge and thank all spiritual beings for their role in this process.

2. Before beginning a session, affirm that the energy to be cleared from a person is being transmuted and transformed. You can visualize the room filled with purifying violet light, or use another appropriate visualization.

    Another visualization you can use is bringing a white sheet up through the floor. As the sheet rises, any imbalanced energy is carried away with it. After the white sheet has passed through the room, affirm that the energies are being transformed. Taking time to do this is well worth the effort in terms of maintaining a balance in your healing environment.

3. After a session, again give thanks and acknowledgment.

4. Periodically clean and charge your healing room crystals.

5. Use sage smoke to purify the area after a healing session. Hold the container with the burning sage and walk around the room, waving the smoke into the four corners and over your healing table or area.

Further Comments on Healing

Although it is not absolutely essential, a person's trust and willingness to work with you are most helpful. However, you may find that the healing energies flowing through you are backing up into your fingers, palms, and wrists. This is an indication that on some level the person is choosing at this time to block the flow of vital life energies. When this happens, you have a responsibility to tell the person that it is not possible for you to do anything more for him or her at this time, and end the session. You must also release any judgmental attitudes about yourself as a healing channel, or any other negative thoughts related to the experience.

Chapter 11

MORE TECHNIQUES FOR CRYSTAL HEALING WITH OTHERS

T his chapter describes some additional ways to use crystals for working with others if you have a larger number of them. They include:

* Triangle grids.
* The 12-point grid.
* Sound and crystals: tuning forks.
* Ideas for massage therapists and body workers.

We will then complete this chapter with some illustrations of crystal arrangements. We experimented with creating a Star of David grid by placing six crystals on pedestals around the healing table. The purpose of this grid is to strengthen the spiritual subtle body and to provide a sacred healing energy pattern for the whole room. Therefore, the crystals in this grid always point toward the healing table. They can be programmed to transmit unconditional love.

We could mention here that we were able to travel to Arkansas and buy clear quartz crystals at a time when they were much less expensive. It is not necessary to have a lot of crystals in order to do effective energy work. Your intent, your spiritual attunement, and the receptiveness to change on the part of the client, are the essential ingredients.

Triangle Grids

These are wonderful healing patterns to use with Herkimer diamonds, or small single-pointed crystals. For clearing, we like the "Y-grid", which encourages an energy flow in the most balanced manner. It is interesting to note that in astrology there is a "Y" aspect pattern called a "yod" which is associated with adjustment, and letting go. The triangle, as we noted earlier, is associated with the Fire element and it stimulates energy movement. At the solar plexus and below you can place them pointing toward the feet, but this is matter of belief and perception, because you can also point them all toward the head. You might place a single crystal on an area that is mildly congested and the Y-grid on an area where there is more blockage or deactivation.

For infusion and expansion you can place them all pointing towards the head. If you want to build up strength or power, point the crystals inward.

The 12-Point Grid

This pattern consists of five pairs of crystals that are placed outside the major joints of the body. Crystals are placed on each side of the neck, shoulders, hips, knees, and ankles. Major joints often become congested with stress and tension, so crystals can play a vital role in clearing and infusing these areas. We also place one or two crystals at the feet, and one at the head. You can turn these crystals according to how you wish to mentally direct the energy. For example:

Figures 11-2 and 11-4 show a crystal at the sending foot for clearing. You can visualize energy being released through this foot. You can also affirm that energy is being released from the top of the head, and use a crystal to amplify this flow.

In the infusion, Figures 11-3 and 11-5, we add a crystal to the receiving foot, or you can place a crystal between both feet. Sensitive people tend to find a head crystal pointed toward the body uncomfortable, so we usually always point the crystal away from the body.

In Figure 11-6, the spiritual expansion grid directs the energy flow from the feet to the head.

Using Tuning Forks for Sound Healing

A potent way of working with sound for healing is to order a set of thirteen tuning forks from your local music store. Here are two ways to use them:

1. Determine either intuitively or by using your voice, a tone needed for a specific area of the body. Place a clearing crystal or "Y-grid" on the area. Strike the appropriate tuning fork on a wooden block, your knee, or other hard surface, to activate the vibration. Hold the tuning fork over the crystals. You will learn to sense when the flow is restored. Do not strike the tuning fork on a stone, because over time, this will change the tone of the tuning fork.

2. Use the tuning fork like a crystal, and rotate it above the chakras or with your alignment of crystals.

Ideas for Massage Therapists and Bodyworkers

1. You can work inside a crystal grid or place crystals or clusters under your healing table. You can also place crystals in the corners of the room, with the points facing the center.

2. You can tape crystals to the tops of your hands, pointing toward the fingertips, to amplify the life force energy flowing through your hands.

3. A crystal that has been rounded at one end is effective when pressed on the acupressure points and foot reflexology zones to clear blocked energy.

4. We have found that clearing blocked energy from tight muscles reduces the time necessary to massage the muscle.

Y-grid for clearing the lower three chakras

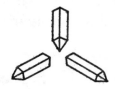

Y-grid for clearing the upper four chakras

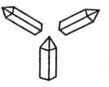

Y-grid for infusing

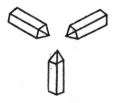

Y-grid for spiritual expansion

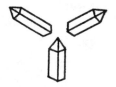

Figure 11-1: Y-grids

You first use the clearing position to restore energy flow, then massage the muscle, and finally follow with the infusing position.

5. Another clearing method that one can use at the beginning of a massage session is holding the crystal between both hands, pointing down toward the body. Roll the crystal back and forth between your hands across the body until you have covered the entire energy field.

6. To continue the clearing process, place your receiving hand on or above a congested area. Holding a crystal in your sending hand, point toward the fingertips, rotate the crystal counterclockwise in the air, away from the client's body. Continue rotating until the area feels cleared.

7. To infuse energy, hold your receiving hand in the air and hold a crystal in your sending hand, rotating it counterclockwise over the intended area, visualizing life force energy coming through the crystal into the client's body. Continue until you sense that the area has received enough energy.

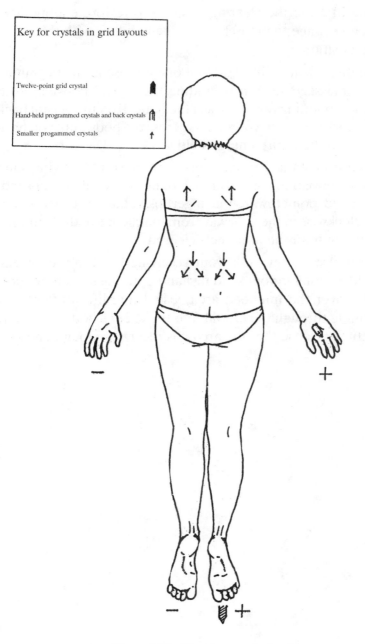

Key for crystals in grid layouts

Twelve-point grid crystal

Hand-held programmed crystals and back crystals

Smaller progammed crystals

Figure 11-2. Clearing on the back.

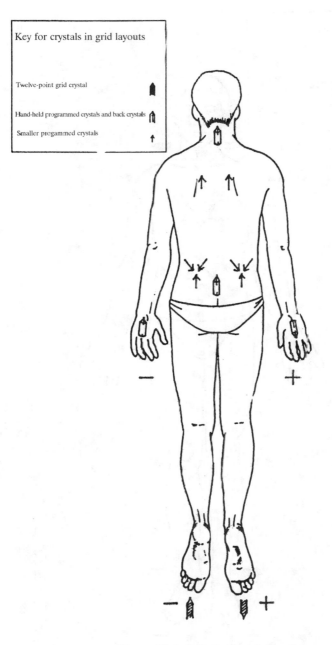

Figure 11-3. Infusing on the back.

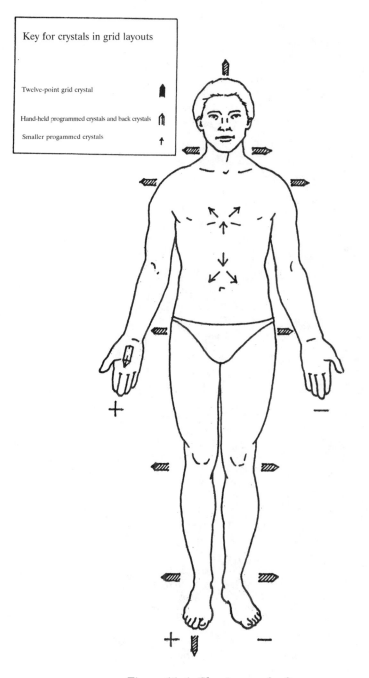

Figure 11-4. Clearing on the front.

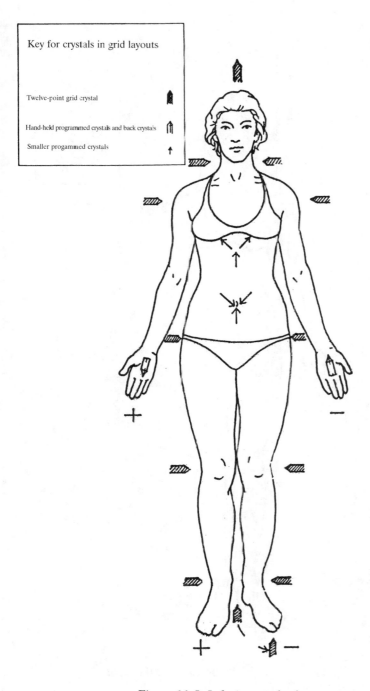

Key for crystals in grid layouts

Twelve-point grid crystal

Hand-held programmed crystals and back crystals

Smaller progammed crystals

Figure 11-5. Infusing on the front.

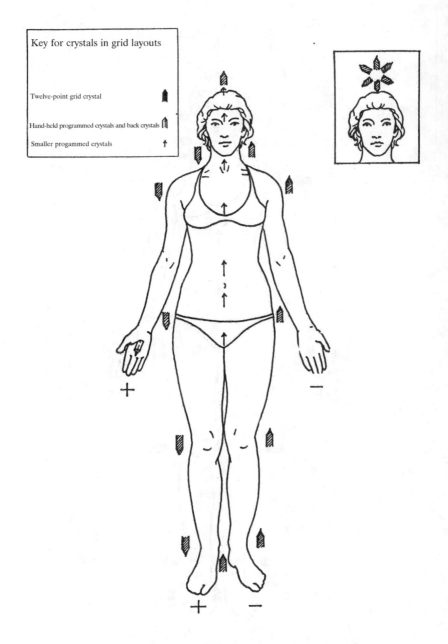

Key for crystals in grid layouts

Twelve-point grid crystal

Hand-held programmed crystals and back crystals

Smaller progammed crystals

Figure 11-6. Spiritual expansion on the front.

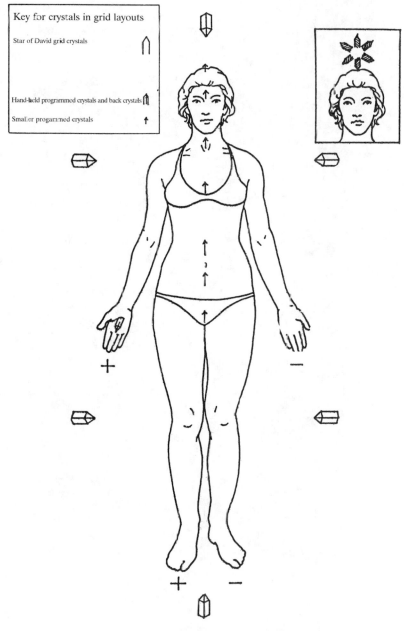

Key for crystals in grid layouts

Star of David grid crystals

Hand-held programmed crystals and back crystals

Smaller progarmmed crystals

Figure 11-7. The Star of David Crystal Grid.

Chapter 12

PLANETARY HEALING

I n Chapter 1 we explained how everything is composed of life force energy. All forms in the physical universe are complex, organized patterns of life force energy. As you begin to work with crystals you will realize that life force energy is conscious energy. In fact, in many eastern traditions, this all-pervading, creative energy is called "consciousness." In these traditions, consciousness and life force energy are understood to be inseparable—like two sides of the same coin. One cannot exist without the other.

It is the nature of consciousness to exist in a state of interconnectedness and constant evolution. Everything in the universe exists at varying levels of consciousness. On a physical level, consciousness is the harmonious interaction of each cell and molecule to maintain the balance of the whole. On a spiritual level, we experience consciousness as unconditional love, balance, harmony, and peace, as well as a constant process of change. Human beings, quartz crystals, and everything else in Nature have their own individual consciousness that evolves toward the fulfillment of its pattern of growth, on both the physical and spiritual levels. In the following channelings, the Crystal

Deva elaborates on this theme:

"As the human kingdom grows through life's experiences and through changes of physical vehicles, I too am evolving, for I was created from the same spark of energy as was the human kingdom. I retain and store knowledge within my being just as the human kingdom stores memory. You see, my capacity for storing knowledge is infinitely greater than that of the human kingdom, because the human kingdom has chosen to perceive itself as more limited in different ways. Creative expression is a vitally important aspect of my work and is important at this time, for I am a catalyst to help pull the human kingdom out of its limits, to see a greater reality, to enable humanity to tap into the far reaches of the infinite cosmos."

We can learn much about unconditional love and other qualities such as patience and trust by attuning with Nature's kingdoms.

"I have the ability to instill confidence and courage in all who choose to work with me, for where there is even a seed of those qualities, I have the capacity to expand them within you to their highest ultimate form. Know that it is impossible to hate or fear when you have come into pure connection with me, for I am a channel of pure unconditional love and light for the human king-dom as well as all other kingdoms. (That is why my energies are so well received by the plant kingdoms.) I can enable you to speak with pure truth, with clarity and understanding in all situations and experiences that unfold in life."

Each crystal has a higher purpose to serve, which can be ascertained either by sitting receptively with the crystal and attuning with it or by using a pendulum. Although there are some sources that classify crystals according to their function, we find that you can limit the wisdom crystals can teach you by imposing a set of characteristics or descriptions upon them. Here are some questions that can help you receive intuitive guidance about a crystal's purpose.

1. "Is your highest function to restore harmony and balance on the physical, emotional, or mental levels of my being?" (Healing.)

a. "Can you be placed on the physical body?"

b. "Are you to work with clearing negative thoughts?"

2. "Is your highest function to expand the light within my higher spiritual levels?" (Meditation.)

3. "Is your highest purpose related to planetary healing?"

4. "Is it for your highest good to be used for devic or other interdimensional communication?"

5. "Do you have stored symbols or other knowledge inside you to be accessed receptively?"

6. "Is it for your highest good to be used in a technological capacity or in a grid system as a transmitter?

Above all, it is important to remember that any time you work with a crystal to assist your spiritual growth, or to be of service to others, you are fulfilling both your own higher purpose and that of the crystal.

Planetary Healing

Consciousness, or life force energy, is our very life. We are both made of it and sustained by it. It is important to recognize our interconnectedness with the whole spectrum of life force energies, from the Earth's geomagnetic energy field to higher spiritual consciousness. We need food, air, and water to live. We also need the nourishment of love in order to live—a love that is based on a balance of giving and receiving. As we learn to express our interconnectedness and love in more and more ways, we evolve and make many changes in this process. We change as we explore different levels of knowledge. We learn that the quality of our thoughts and actions affects our own life, the lives of others, and the planet as well, since we are the Earth and the Earth is us. Planetary healing becomes a way of life, because planetary healing is life.

In this book we have focused on how transforming our thoughts changes the quality of the life force energy that we receive and utilize in our personal healing. Working with our thoughts is a form of planetary healing, because the life force energy expressed in our thoughts becomes part of the life energy, or consciousness, that sustains the physical and spiritual aspects of our planet. In the following channelings, the

Crystal Deva talks about the Devic kingdom and how the devas work with thought forms:

"My kingdom is based in the world of spirit. We devas have no physical structure as you do. We are 'light beings' with light bodies that are essentially formless. Our will is the will of the Divine, whereas you have both a personal will and the higher will of the Divine. You communicate primarily on the verbal level where we utilize thought based in pure knowingness. You have a powerful effect on your earth plane reality since you live within a physical vehicle, on the earth plane. You work with the physical form of things. We operate in the realm of life force energies that are without physical structure. Our purpose is to create the reality of physical form through our work with life force energies. In our dimension time and space are infinite. Everything is. We communicate directly with infinite light and wisdom. It is the same as your being at one with your higher self-essence. We seek a greater expansion and knowingness of spirit, as you do. We work without emotional considerations of our actions, knowing that we are eternally linked to the light....

"I am a deva for the clear crystal blueprint. There are also overlighting devas that create the blueprint of balance for a geographical area. The number of different life forms involved, and the extent that we receive human cooperation in maintaining balance, determines the size of the area.

"We work to maintain balance within the life forms that have been created physically on or within the earth's surface. We continue to transmit new energized forms that are created from life force energy.

"Positive human thought forms increase the quality of life force energy that permeates the elements of the planet. This results in normal, healthy growth cycles for all of Nature's kingdoms. We do not rely solely on positive human thought energies in our work. But the more positive the energy that has been transmitted from the human kingdom, the more we can sustain the existing balance of energy on the planet.

"When we are aware of a negative human group thought form, we surround it with white light so that no further expansion of that thought form can take place. We then focus light towards its center to transform its energies into a neutralized state. We also begin work at the outer layers of the form, again with focused white light. Change takes place as the layers take on greater light. Once the thought form has been totally neutralized, then the encircling light is removed because it is no longer needed. The form is charged with life force energies by imprinting a perfect pattern on it, and then it is transmitted for use in planetary balance.

"We also work in an orderly manner with each positive group thought form, such as the ones created on December 31, and on the solstices and equinoxes. We sense its different vibrational levels, or layers, to determine where the planet can optimally utilize the energy. We then accompany each vibrational level to its destination and infuse its light into the appropriate energy field for healing and balance.

"Not every group thought form is dispersed throughout the entire planet. We have maintained the positive group thought form energies manifested at the time of the harmonic convergence according to the higher guidance that we receive. Its presence serves as a 'guiding light channel' for those of the human kingdom that are moving into higher levels of consciousness."

Using Crystals for Planetary Healing

There are several ways you can use crystals for planetary healing:

1. When working individually, you can hold a crystal and see planet Earth as totally healed and vibrantly alive, with all her kingdoms in perfect order and balance. This thought will merge with others of similar vibrational frequency, and the crystal will also amplify your thoughts. It is not so much the particular thought content, but the quality of your compassion that makes the difference.

2. When you decide to go to a natural area, take quartz crystal with you. It comes from the Earth and feels right at home. Through your thoughts send unconditional love to the kingdoms of Nature around you. Your thoughts can be used to help balance the natural area you are in.

3. The veins of quartz crystal serve a significant function in transforming and stabilizing the energies that flow from the Earth's core to the surface. In many locations quartz crystal is being mined without consideration for the imbalance it may be creating in Mother Earth.

   Merge with your crystal and visualize yourself in a cave with myriads of beautiful crystal clusters and points. Travel through the cave, feeling the balance and clarity of the crystals. The cave stretches on to become veins of crystal under the earth. Visualize waves of balanced, clear crystal energy flowing like light through the veins, spreading under the surface of the earth.

4. Consider working with a group for planetary healing. You can do a healing meditation in which each person holds a crystal in the sending hand and focuses healing thoughts to a crystal grid or a single crystal in the center. The center crystal can represent the Earth, and it will also amplify the power of group focus.

5. We have also used a world map as a way of focusing energy. Each person can hold a crystal in the sending hand for amplification, and place another crystal on the map where he or she wishes to send healing energy. You can also place crystals on sacred places like the pyramids in Egypt. Each person focuses healing energy and peace to a particular spot in the world, and then to the planet as a whole.

"Changes on the planet are accelerating, both in your personal lives, and in the kingdoms of Nature. Change is a natural part of the growth process, and you have a choice in how you respond to change. You can best co-create with spirit by seeking to comprehend the messages that underlie your experiences. Responsible stewardship means that the human kingdom must bring itself into a greater alignment with the kingdoms of Nature and

with Mother Earth. Seek to be a clear channel of light by acting according to the highest good, as you perceive it to be. The crystal kingdom continues to be a catalyst through which you can better understand what it means to live in alignment with your own highest purpose, and with the planet."

ENDNOTES

Chapter 1:

1. Kenneth Cohen, "Bones of Our Ancestors," *Yoga Journal 60* (1985), p. 56.
2. Judith Larkin, Ph.D., "Counseling With Crystals," in John Vincent Milewski and Virginia L. Harford, eds., *The Crystal Sourcebook* (Santa Fe: Mystic Crystal Publications, 1987), pp. 263-265.
3. Ibid., p. 266.
4. Edmund Harold, *Focus on Crystals* (New York: Ballantine Books, 1986), p. 5.
5. Ibid., pp. 9-10.
6. John Vincent Milewski, Ph.D., "Herkimer Diamonds," in John Vincent Milewski and Virginia L. Harford, eds., *The Crystal Sourcebook* (Santa Fe: Mystic Publications, 1987), p. 217.

Chapter 3:

1. Randall Baer and Vicki Baer, *Windows of Light* (New York: Harper & Row, 1984), p. 60.

Chapter 6:

1. Gabriel Cousens, M.D., *Spiritual Nutrition and the Rainbow Diet* (Boulder: Cassandra Press, 1986), p. 37.
2. Ibid., p. 49.

3. Ibid., p. 81.

4. Ibid., p. 89.

5. Randall Baer and Vicki Baer, *The Crystal Connection* (New York: Harper & Row, 1986), p. 343.

6. Aubrey Westlake, *The Pattern of Health* (New York: Devin-Adair Co., 1963), p. 35.

7. Ibid., p. 36.

Chapter 7:

Darius Dinshah, *Let There Be Light* (Dinshah Health Society, PO Box 707, Malaga, NJ, 03828), p. 95.

BIBLIOGRAPHY

Alper, the Reverend Dr. Frank. *Exploring Atlantis, Vols. I and II.* Phoenix: Arizona Metaphysical Society, 1982.

Baer, Randall N., and Vicki B. *Windows of Light.* New York: Harper & Row Publishers, Inc., 1984.

Baer, Randall N., and Vicki B. *The Crystal Connection.* New York: Harper & Row Publishers, Inc., 1986.

Burke, George. *Magnetic Therapy.* Oklahoma City: Saint George Press, 1980.

Lantieri, Linda, and Elaine Seiler. *Quartz Crystal, A Gift From the Earth.* Northhampton: Resource Management Ltd., 1985.

Laskow, Leonard, M.D., *Healing with Love.* San Francisco: Harper and Row Publishers, Inc., 1992.

Logan, Elizabeth A. *A Crystal Cosmos Network Directory.* Winnipeg: Crystal Cosmos Network, 1986.

Milewski, John Vincent, and Virginia L. Harford. *The Crystal Sourcebook.* Santa Fe: Mystic Crystal Publications, 1987.

Nielson, Greg, and Joseph Polasky. *Pendulum Power.* New York: Warner Books, 1977.

Raphaell, Katrina. *Crystal Enlightenment.* New York: Aurora Press, 1985.

Small, Jacqueline. *Transformers, the Therapists of the Future.* Marina del Rey: De Vorss and Company, 1982.

Walker, Dael. *The Crystal Book.* Sunol: The Crystal Company, 1983.

Westlake, Aubrey. *The Pattern of Health.* New York: Devon-Adair Co., 1963.

INDEX

ABOUT THE AUTHORS

Pamela L. Chase, M.S., and Jonathan Pawlik have been working with the mineral kingdom as healers and counselors for more than 15 years, and crystals have played a key role in their own healing journey. They are also the co-authors of *Healing with Gemstones* and *Trees for Healing.*